D1298615

0 11557 03193   5

INTRODUCING
YOUR KIDS
to the
OUTDOORS

INTRODUCING
YOUR KIDS
to the
OUTDOORS

Christopher Van Tilburg, M.D.

STACKPOLE
BOOKS

Published by
STACKPOLE BOOKS
5067 Ritter Road
Mechanicsburg, PA 17055
www.stackpolebooks.com

Printed in U.S.A.

First edition

10 9 8 7 6 5 4 3 2 1

All photos, including cover photo, copyright 2005 by Christopher Van Tillburg except those on pages 30, 68, 92, 98, 102, and 141, copyright 2005 by Clint Bogard (www.gorgelight.com), and pages 5, 66, 134, 135, 142, 144, and 150, copyright 2005 by Jonathan Ciambotti.

Cover design by Wendy A. Reynolds

Library of Congress Cataloging-in-Publication Data

Van Tilburg, Christopher.
   Introducing your kids to the outdoors / Christopher Van Tilburg.—1st ed.
      p. cm.
   Includes index.
   ISBN 0-8117-3193-6 (alk. paper)
   1. Outdoor recreation for children. 2. Family recreation. I. Title.
   GV191.63.V36 2005
   796'.083—dc22

2004013893

For my parents, Wayne and Eleanor,
and my children, Skylar and Avrie

Contents

Preface

My earliest childhood memory is of learning to ski. I was four years old and I remember the gray overcast sky and the blanket of white snow that covered our yard and cow pasture. I grew up in a small town along the shores of the Columbia River, where we received one or two days of snow annually. When it snowed, school was canceled and businesses were closed. Dad would stay home from work. Mom would make cinnamon rolls. It was pure delight.

Mom bundled me in my warmest clothes and strapped on my red rubber rain boots. Dad hauled out the long red skis that he had bought in Europe. Once outside, Dad clicked his leather lace-up ski boots into the bindings. I stood on top of the skis just in front of Dad's boots. He held me by the armpits and we sped down the cow pasture straight for the barn. The snow was thick and gooey, but it didn't matter. It was exhilarating. The cool, damp wind blew in my face and a floating feeling intoxicated me the way a roller coaster does. The thrill settled not in my stomach but somewhere deeper in my heart. I don't know how many runs we made, but I remember walking back into our warm house, peeling off my cold, wet layers, and huddling in front of the fireplace with a cup of hot chocolate, a ritual that would become a wonderful part of my childhood. I'm sure I had a grin as wide as the skis were long.

Throughout my childhood, I have fond memories of family ski trips. I remember sleeping in my long underwear the night before we went skiing. I remember the seemingly endless days in the high mountain sun and clear air. I remember the exotic ski towns of Canada, Europe, and America.

After years of skiing, I picked up snowboarding in the early days of the sport. I traveled around the world, climbing and snowboarding big peaks, and eventually wrote books on ski and snowboard mountaineering.

Before either of my daughters were able to walk, I had a deep-seated desire to head to the mountains with them. I skied down the gentle beginner slopes with both my kids in the child-carry backpack. The rush of wind brought smiles to their faces. I've come full circle and enjoyed every minute of it.

When Skylar, my oldest daughter, was one and a half, we bought a pair of 80 cm skis and size 7 boots at our local ski swap. We hadn't intended to do much skiing that year. But when we were on a spring ski trip with my extended family, Skylar wanted to ski with her cousins, who were a few years older. On a warm sunny day, we helped Skylar into her skis and set out for an adventure.

At first, we held her between our legs and cruised down the slope. But after a few days we got a harness. On the first few runs we held her close, but over the course of a week we gradually let the lines out. Flanked by her cheering cousins, Skylar would point her skis straight down the hill and laugh—or more often sing "Do-Re-Mi" from *The Sound of Music*—while feeling gravity's pull. We didn't push it. We only went on sunny days and well before lunch time. We always had plenty of snacks and even a few treats. Usually we made three or four runs on the beginner slope, took a break, made two more runs, and then called it a day.

We did have tough days. Once back home, after half an hour of packing and another driving to the mountain, we realized we were too close to lunch and naptime. We pushed it: big mistake. After three minutes in the skis, Skylar was screaming and crying. We had lunch and drove home. Skylar fell asleep before we got out of the parking lot. More often, though, we go with friends, and it is a big party. A few runs with snacks on the chairlift, lunch with friends, and a drive home during naptime seemed to work pretty well. We always play lots of games, laugh, and cheer.

Now Skylar skis the whole mountain with confidence and enthusiasm. My second daughter, Avrie, rips at an early age too, especially from watching her older sister. You'd think it was twice the challenge: two sets of gear, two mouths to feed, two naps to contend with. But Skylar helps get her own gear ready and packs the lunch. Avrie makes tracks as big as her smile. The small effort is hugely gratifying, not only to see them excel at a sport in the high alpine world but for them to follow my tracks. In just a few years, they will be ripping just as fast as me. Maybe the girls will pick up snowboarding, and maybe they will climb mountains with me. I have no doubt that they, too, will sleep in ski clothes the night before a trip.

Acknowledgments

First and foremost, I need to thank my parents, Wayne and Eleanor Van Tilburg. Our family spent many days of my childhood and early adult life fishing, hunting, skiing, camping, and traveling abroad. Dad and Mom always put our family first. My children, Skylar and Avrie, and my wife, Jennifer, have been troopers every step of the way in our own outdoor adventures.

I have worked with many equipment companies on this and many other projects. Specifically, I used the following family- or child-specific outdoor equipment: Baby Jogger running stroller; Boeri ski and snowboard helmets; Coleman family first aid kits; Columbia Sportswear clothing; Dakine backpacks, hats, and gloves; ET America first aid kits; Giro ski and snowboard helmets; K2 snowboards; Kelty tents and sleeping bags; L.L. Bean clothing; Mountain Safety Research tents; Adams Trail-a-bike tandem bikes; Sawyer kids' first aid kits; Smartwool clothing; Patagonia clothing; The North Face tents and sleeping bags; Trail-gator bike tow bars; WPC Brands family first aid kits; and Yakima bike racks, cargo boxes, and child bike trailers.

My colleagues and friends read many of these pages. Many thanks to Mark Nykanen, for advice, friendship, and family trips. Dee Holtzman and Jon Ciambotti made excellent contributions. Clint Bogard (www.gorge light.com) and Jon Ciambotti graciously provided photos. Jessica Lichtenstein and Joelle Delbourgo at Joelle Delbourgo Associates provided support and enthusiasm for this project. Many thanks to the crew at Stackpole, including Judith Schnell and Amy Lerner.

THE BASICS

When I have an idea for a camping trip, a day hike, or even a quick trip to the river, my daughters get excited. Skylar runs for a pencil and paper so she can start making a list: food, equipment, clothing, friends to invite. Avrie wants to pack her bag right that minute and put her bike helmet or swimsuit on. They are wild kids; they love outdoor adventure. Part mentor, friend, coach, and parent, I love introducing them to the wonder of nature and the thrill of outdoor sports. From my perspective as a physician, outdoor sports expert, and parent, I will share the tools you need to take your own wild kids outside in the sun, wind, rain, or snow. You will learn the deep satisfaction and thrilling excitement of adventuring and traveling with your family.

Part 1 presents the fundamental knowledge for getting started, namely, how to plan, pack, organize, and assemble. Don't be overwhelmed: Family outdoor adventures can be simple and straightforward, without too much effort or hassle, and even without spending too much money. I've eliminated much of the mystery and headache and focused on the important issues. I've attempted nearly everything in this book either as a child or as a parent. I've gathered advice from other outdoor expert parents as well, so rest assured, these ideas and techniques will work.

Read through the basics first, and then have your son or daughter start a list of activities. You're in for a thrill of a lifetime and a rewarding journey.

The Dynamics of Adventure

The planning and packing for our first camping trip of the season begin weeks in advance. We pick out a campground on the Oregon coast and block out a few days on our hectic schedule. Before the trip, we set up the tent in the backyard for a test run picnic. My kids are brimming with excitement and enthusiasm. My oldest daughter Skylar writes the grocery list, and we stop by the camp supply store for propane, batteries, plates, and a spare flashlight. My youngest Avrie is revved up, although not exactly sure what is going on. The night before we leave, I let my daughters pack their small clothing bags. After they fall asleep, I check to make sure that they have enough socks and underwear and that they brought pants instead of dresses. In the morning, we load up our big gray Suburban, affectionately called Gorilla, with all the essentials: rubber boots, raincoats, warm clothes, bikes and helmets, sunscreen, swimsuits, sun hats, warm hats, sleeping bags, pillows, camp gear, soccer balls, and the stuffed animals.

We leave town despite the forecast of rain. On the road, we have lots of activities for Skylar and Avrie: crayons, books, art kits, dolls. We listen to the *Shrek* soundtrack for about the hundredth time. "Are we there yet?" and "How much longer?" questions start in about ten minutes after we leave town.

At Cape Lookout campground on the Oregon coast, the sky is clear and cloudless. The warm sea breeze drifts in over the sand dunes. My daughters are delighted; my wife and I are too. We pull into our campsite, then run on the beach and play in the gentle, but frigid, waves. Later we set up camp, including our two tents. The play/dressing/storage tent usually gets full of sand and mud: That's what I set it up for. The sleep tent is reserved for quiet time and sleeping: no shoes. We set up our deluxe camp kitchen and a solar heated shower in about fifteen minutes; we're pro campers by now.

Then we're off again: biking the campground loop, wading in the gentle shore break, hiking the campground's one-mile interpretive trail, exploring tide pools, and building sand castles. At night we grill chicken and hot dogs on the campfire and then roast marshmallows for s'mores. At dark, we snuggle in our warm tent. I read a few books to my daughters, and then we turn off our flashlights, watch the stars through the tent skylight, and drift into deep peaceful sleep.

The next day is more of the same nonstop action. On day three, though, we wake up to a downpour. We're still dry and cozy in our tent, but rain puddles collect in our campsite. I cook oatmeal in the rain, and then we have breakfast in the tent. We stuff the soggy camp gear into the Gorilla. On the way home, we stop at an ice cream stand.

I deem the trip a veritable success gauged by chocolate ice cream smiles on my kids' faces, and their cries of "I don't want to go home," when we pull into our driveway.

WHY OUTDOOR SPORTS?

Introducing your children to outdoor adventure sports can be thrilling, educational, and wondrous. You might be camping at your favorite coast campground, hiking a local trail, or rock climbing at the school wall. A wilderness medicine colleague of mine took his two kids trekking across Bhutan, but a regular activity for my family is riding on our local bike path.

The first question—and you may sound like your child—is "Why?" Parents often ask me why they should drag their children into the jungles, mountains, forests, oceans, and deserts of the world. The immediate benefits are readily apparent: The air is clean, the fun is wholesome, and the exercise is good for their physical and mental health. Kids will eat better, sleep better, and perform better at school and social functions. Children learn a tremendous amount from outdoor sports and adventure travel. They can study the natural world, wilderness ecosystems, plant and animal habitats, and other sciences ranging from ecology to orienteering (route-finding with a map and compass). In short, outdoor adventure sports give kids a healthy and complementary alternative to learning in a classroom setting.

When they hear about my escapades with my own children, parents often ask me, "Isn't it dangerous?" The quick and easy answer is generally, no. Realistically, the downside of outdoor adventure is minor. The main outdoor hazard is foul weather, and the chief potential physical problem is injury from a fall. I continually emphasize safety so that injury and environmental hazards are minimized and, in many cases, nearly eliminated. The activities I will discuss and demonstrate are very safe; I never place my

Take your time. Kids are fascinated with anything, even a newt.

family in potentially harmful or dangerous situations. I'll show you how to avoid them too.

We want our kids to be safe and stay healthy, but we don't want to restrict their learning opportunities. Nor do we want to shelter them so much that they don't learn how to fall and get back up again. Thus as we begin discussing parenting, you will begin to see it largely as an act of balance. You will learn to balance exploration with safety and enthusiasm with caution.

Let's look at the psychosocial, educational, and physical benefits of outdoor sports in more detail.

HEALTHY BRAINS = HEALTHY KIDS

Outdoor adventure sports are a fantastic setting for kids to explore, learn, and play. They provide a perfect opportunity for you to interact with your children: teaching them, bonding with them, and learning from them. The natural world promotes positive cognitive development, increasingly important in a world that is dominated by computers, television, and other sedentary activities. In fact, spontaneous playtime outside is now recognized as one of the most important ways a child learns and develops, especially in today's world where educational videos, electronic learning toys, and computer teaching programs are omnipresent in our children's lives. Kids will learn independence, good behavior, responsibility, self-reliance, and cooperation from outdoor activities.

All kids approach outdoor sports in much the same manner. They base their willingness to proceed or their decision to give up mostly on internal satisfaction and gratification with physical activity in the outdoor environment. Simply put, it must be fun or kids will lose interest and motivation. Fun is a broad term that for older kids might also include a physical or mental challenge, learning a new sport or skills, friendly competition, achieving goals, and physical exertion. Moreover, learning about the natural world can be fascinating and inspiring; it broadens kids' learning environment and varies their life experiences. In fact, some will find their life's work as a result of this early exposure, whether it is in athletics, nature, science, or travel.

Experts say that important developmental milestones are fostered by outdoor sports. Children can establish strong self-esteem and reduce their sense of helplessness. Outdoor activities improve a child's idea of control, self-determination, and autonomy. Kids learn independence, self-reliance, decision-making, and responsibility. This is perhaps most important for older children, for whom outdoor activities are an opportunity to escape the stress of home or school without resorting to less desirable, or even dangerous, alternatives. In short, outdoor adventure sports build character and strong, smart, healthy kids.

Many parents ask me about safety concerns in the outdoors, and with good reason. Fear of the outdoors has both physical and psychological implications. It is important to teach your child to employ respect and caution in the natural world and, in some situations, to be fearful. Most child psychologists agree that if you say, "Be careful!" too many times, however, it could have undesirable effects. On one hand, a young child may become fearful of every activity. With too much fear, kids may miss out on the experience, and they may develop obsessions or even aversions to outdoor sports and nature in general. On the other hand, with overcautious parents, older kids may be fearful of nothing when they realize that many times the fear is unfounded or exaggerated. You will need to find a balance that works for you and your children.

THE OUTDOOR CLASSROOM

Most children spend nearly all of their formal learning in a classroom. This style of learning is an important part of child development, but the outdoor world is complementary to indoor classrooms. Instead of learning from a passive, controlled setting, outdoor kids learn from active, physical stimulation that is neither completely controlled nor absolutely predictable. They will develop a new framework for experiences, and they will also gain a broader understanding of the world around them.

Let's look at two grade-school kids, Charlie and Janelle. When Charlie sees a spider in the house, he asks his mom to smash it because "spiders make cobwebs and then we have to clean them up." This is how Charlie interacts with spiders mostly because this is how he learned to deal with them—indoors and on a limited basis.

When Janelle saw a moth in the window she asked her dad to put it outside. "That's where its home is," she said. She was excited, not from fear, but because she knew the moth would rather live outside. Janelle learned that moths have a necessary and fundamental role and that they are important in the circle of life. She built upon that experience when she saw a butterfly, the moth's cousin, perched on a flower at the park. "They help the plants grow," her dad told her. Later, while on a nature walk, she saw a caterpillar, cocoon, and butterfly at different points on the trail; she began to understand the circle of life and why we respect nature. Janelle told all the kids at school that they shouldn't smash caterpillars because they become butterflies.

Let's look at another example. Charlie has spent most of his formative years in school. His concepts of animals, for example, come mainly from his pet cat Bob and through teachers, books, and television. He knows most animals by name and can mimic their voices. However, the concepts are somewhat blunted and two dimensional. When he sees animals in the wild, he becomes timid and sometimes afraid. He is unsure just how to interact with them. He is overly cautious and slightly fearful.

Janelle attends school but also spends many weekends with her family outdoors. She has learned both from traditional means as well as through nature hikes, beach walks, and bike rides. She has seen bird nests, beaver dams, and foraging deer. Once she saw a family of skunks with six young strolling through the campground. Unlike Charlie, Janelle was enthusiastic but respectful when she came across the skunks. Despite their foul odor, she didn't scowl. "Be very quiet," she said to her father as she watched from a distance. "They are looking for their lunch."

The natural world comes to life for Janelle; she sees it in three dimensions. She learns respect, admiration, and the places of different animals and plants in the circle of life. This broad learning environment gives her more experiences and knowledge to build upon.

Kids get formal instruction and playtime indoors for much of their lives. Outdoor sports and activities are a chance to let them develop person-

We search for tadpoles.

alities and behaviors that are more adaptive to a greater number of chal-lenges and that are based on broader experiences. Remember, parental involvement is an essential ingredient, as I'll discuss throughout this book.

Yes, kids do need balance: Too much outdoor stimulation makes it diffi-cult to return to school. My wife and I found that three-day weekends are a perfect getaway, and for extended trips in summer or during winter break, fourteen days is the most we like to be gone. That gives us enough time away, but we're not gone so long that the kids get bored or have trouble get-ting back into the routine of home.

Outdoor education instructors point out several additional elements that are essential to outdoor education:

- Teach respect and value of different environments, whether moun-tains and snow, the beach and ocean, or a local park. Teach kids not to kill spiders, because they perform an important function in the circle

Good thing we brought boots for this tadpole search.

of life (namely, capturing those pesky flies). For more detailed information, see the section on environmental ethics on pages 12 and 13.

- Teach cultural heritage. This is very important because it provides background for and reinforces knowledge that kids learn in class. For example, it is one thing to read and talk about Lewis and Clark's Corps of Discovery expedition. But if you can complement it with observations like "This is the type of forest where Lewis and Clark may have spent the winter," or questions such as "How do you think you would build a fort like Lewis and Clark's Fort Clatsop?" your child will gain a deeper appreciation, remember lessons in more detail, and become inspired to learn more.

- Teach how the natural world works. Teach kids that bees don't just sting and make nests, but they pollinate flowers to help them grow.

My daughter first didn't like the rain—it made her wet, she said. However, when I told her that rain made trees grow and flowers bloom, she gained some respect and admiration for the rain. (Because we live in Oregon, my kids must love rain.)

- Try problem-solving in an uncontrolled environment. This is a key element of learning, especially for older kids. Children need to learn that it's okay to be caught in a rainstorm or to get an "owie" in the woods. This is crucial to developing skills beyond what can be taught in the classroom. Kids learn respect for Mother Nature in the outdoors, especially weather and the risk of getting lost. You don't have to be in the backcountry to teach these lessons; it can be done at your local park, nature preserve, or woodland. At a Wilderness Medical Society conference one year, we had a special segment for kids. We let them alternate playing victims and rescuers to learn how to take care of ill and injured people. Younger kids became less fearful of "owies;" older kids gained confidence to open a first aid kit and lend a hand.

LIFELONG HEALTHY HABITS

There are numerous physical benefits of outdoor sports. Kids get in shape and learn important basic sports skills like running, throwing, swimming, and hiking. They breathe fresh air and get away from the television, telephone, and computer. Plus this form of play does not borrow from board games, toys, or puzzles, but rather from the natural world of forests, mountains, or beaches. Most parents soon realize that with activity, their children will sleep better and eat better.

Moreover, kids will develop a lifelong interest in physical activity, a difficult issue with the sometimes sedentary adult population of today. My wife and I take our kids to gymnastics so they can learn how to tumble, fall, balance, and dance. It is a great opportunity for them to be physical and develop important skills. But we foster these skills outdoors, too, in a safe environment. My daughters practice their balance beam skills on logs when we go on hikes. Logs have irregularities like knots and bark, and they are sometimes slippery with morning dew. These irregularities show my kids that things in nature are not always as controlled as in the gym. Irregularity and unpredictability can be the norm. My girls build upon their gymnastic skills in the forest so when they return to the balance beam, they invariably do better.

There are three important components to physical activity:

1. Cardiovascular fitness, gained from hiking, walking, running, biking, or swimming, is the mainstay for long-term health. It improves

We launch across the river.

the function of the heart and lungs by providing regular, prolonged exercise. Fortunately, most kids get lots of exercise even at the nearest park.

2. Extended hikes or bike rides or power sports like skiing are important for strength and endurance. They keep muscles strong and in good shape. My kids notice when their legs get tired on the first ski day of the season or the first day of summer soccer league.

3. Improved flexibility, agility, and coordination come from skill sports and activities such as skiing or balancing on a log at the park.

All this physical activity should be accompanied with safety. The chief hazard facing outdoor kids, one that I write about often in my work as a wilderness physician, is injury. Parents are commonly worried, and rightly so, about falls or about weather-related ailments like hypothermia. Although much of this book is devoted to safety, one key element is of paramount

Respecting the Natural World

Once, my daughters and I were walking along the riverbank, and we came upon a family of mallard ducks. When the ducks waddled to the water we saw that they had left behind an egg tucked in a clump of grass. Skylar said, "Let's go get it, I want to touch it." My youngest, Avrie, ran to grab the egg. Much to their dismay, we slowly and quietly crept away so the ducks could return to their nest. I spent the next ten minutes telling my daughters over and over why we couldn't pick up the egg or get too close to the nest. It was quite difficult to explain to young girls, but I think they began to understand respect when I told them that was the ducks' home and the egg was the ducks' future child. We didn't want to scare them, I said.

As with all aspects of education, it is important to teach our children to have some environmental ethic, a sense of respect and caring about the world in which we live. This is actually a very simple and straightforward task. Below are basic guidelines for low-impact travel and environmental awareness. They are based on the Leave No Trace ethic of outdoor adventure and well recognized by outdoor experts to be crucial to protecting our wild lands.

- Some mantras that you can teach children of all ages are "Take nothing but pictures, leave nothing but footprints, kill nothing but time," and "Pack it in, pack it out." In other words: Don't bring home rocks, shells, or sticks. Never litter.
- Don't kill bugs, even at home. If you have a bug in your house, set it free by putting it outside.
- Plan a trip according to your family's skill level. Trail damage often occurs when people take on bike rides or hikes that are too difficult for their skills.
- When in the wilderness, travel in small groups. We find that going with one other family is the maximum for wilderness areas or fragile terrain. In parks, campgrounds, or nature preserves with wide, well-maintained trails, larger groups are okay. Sometimes campgrounds, even in the backcountry, have group campsites, which lessen impact.

- When planning a trip, check on weather and trail conditions. For example, hiking a trail in muddy conditions often forces us to walk around puddles, thus expanding the trail and trampling plants. Always stay on the trails.
- Always keep bikes on roads or trails designated for such. For example, wilderness areas and national parks allow bikes only on roads or designated bike paths.
- When out and about, it's okay for kids to yell and scream in certain places like campgrounds in midday. That's part of being a child. But when hiking or biking, use soft trail voices so you do not disturb animals. The exception is when hiking in bear country, where you want to make noise when hiking so you don't surprise a bear on the trail.
- Use caution to avoid hiking on fragile moss, lichen, ground cover, wildflowers, or macrobiotic soil (the collection of algae, lichen, and moss that covers sand). Teach respect for plant habitats.
- Respect animals. In general, animals will bother humans only when they feel their home is being invaded, when they are searching for food, or when they are protecting their young. Observe animals, as well as their nests or dens, from a distance.
- Try to leave the land as you find it, especially when stopping for lunch. Don't move rocks or logs; if you must, replace them.
- Try to take a toilet break at the trailhead if you will be heading away from bathroom facilities. Minimize human waste in wilderness areas as much as possible. Always pack out diapers and wet wipes.
- When camping, it's best to concentrate your activity on known trails and designated campsites. In pristine areas that are remote, spread out your impact to minimize damage to fragile meadows or stream banks.
- Keep food, dishwater, and toilet areas at least three hundred feet from streams, lakes, or other sources of water.
- If you make a fire, keep it small and in the designated fire pit. Gather only downed wood that is three inches in diameter or less. Make sure ashes are cold and wet when you turn in for the night.

importance: supervision. Supervision is the cornerstone of safety, and with proper supervision, injuries, while not totally eliminated, can be minimized, for the most part, to minor scrapes and bruises.

In fact, most parents agree that they don't want their children to think they can't hurt themselves. It is important for kids to fall, get scraped and bruised, and then get up and brush themselves off, or as my oldest daughter says, "Shake it off." With proper attention to safety, as highlighted in later chapters, you can limit injuries to minor ones.

The best approach is to teach children to be cautious and respectful and to teach why. For example, I'll say, "Don't put your hand in that dark hole."

"Why?" asks my daughter.

"Because there may be a sleeping animal in there that will get mad if you wake it up. That is its home, and you need to respect it."

"Oh," says my daughter as we move on to the next object of fascination.

The next time we approach a hole, she says, "Why don't we put our hands in there, Papa?" She is proud that she can teach me this tidbit.

"I don't know, why?" I reply, playing her game.

"Because an animal is sleeping there, and that is its home," she says with a smile.

She proceeds to teach her little sister this lesson every time she sees a hole.

ADVENTURE AFOOT: THE FINE ART OF PARENTING

How young should I start my child? What activity should I start with? These are common and reasonable questions I hear from parents who are just starting out. Who should go and what you do are intertwined. In other words, the type of activity you do will largely depend on the ages of your kids and their stages of development. As most parents know, age does not always correlate directly with development. Some kids are more advanced than their peers when it comes to sports. Also, experts say that kids tend to be more developed physically and psychologically than their parents realize. We are always amazed when our child rides a bike without training wheels for the first time or beats us in a sprint.

It is okay, in fact desirable, to get your kids involved in the outdoors from a young age. They will learn that this is a part of your everyday life. Although it is never too late to start, if you try to peel a teenager away from the internet to go hiking, you may have a tough time, especially if it is your first venture into the outdoors. Young children will tell you through words and body language if they are ready for a particular activity.

Most parents will start their children in outdoor sports during their preschool or school-age years, and that's the main target for this book. How-

Don't forget snacks; a big log makes a great stop.

ever, some parents will pick up a new sport when their kids are teenagers. Other parents with lots of enthusiasm and skills will want to start early, so I've addressed that in a separate chapter on infants and toddlers. For the bulk of this book, we'll focus on school-age kids and teenagers, with some overlap into preschool ages. Let's look at these three main groups.

Preschoolers: Easy, Slow, and Flexible

The preschool years are a fun age for parents. Preschoolers have a lot of energy and a lot of curiosity. As all parents know, they are constantly active and require close supervision. They need to have some sense of exploration to satisfy their curiosity, but you need keep them from getting stuck in a patch of poison oak or from riding their bike into a busy parking lot.

From a psychological point of view, preschoolers can be egocentric, so they need lots of attention from parents or peers. They need simple tasks but sometimes switch to new ones readily and sporadically. Parents often need several variations on a single theme to keep them focused on one activity. Often young kids role play or use pretend themes when playing. They enjoy silliness and care mostly about having fun. Sharing might be challenging, but they do have concrete knowledge about right and wrong.

Lycra sunshirt provides protection from sun and warmth in water.

Their comprehension is concrete too: They are very interested in how things look and feel, not how they came to be.

The fine motor skills are still developing in preschool kids, so they need help with complex tasks. They need to eat regularly but can be picky eaters. They need daily naps or quiet time but always greatly resist it. They are too big to be carried for a long time but may insist on it. At any given time, usually when they need to eat or sleep, they can metamorphose into a Tasmanian devil. Sound tough? With careful planning and preparation, as detailed in subsequent chapters, you can have a simple, enjoyable outing every time.

This is an important stage for outdoor families. You want trips to be fun, but they shouldn't be too difficult. You shouldn't become disenchanted with taking your child on an outdoor adventure. When our kids were small, we went on many nature walks, stroller runs, and bike rides; most trips were in our neighborhood, at our local park, or to the river a few miles from our house. We did a lot of car camping too, where we could take myriad amenities of home. Activities should be short and simple. Give kids guidance, but choose only one activity at a time. Don't rush kids if their pace is slow. Laugh a lot and use your imagination. Play games or act silly. Make sure they are having fun, but don't be afraid to enforce the rules.

The keys for a terrific time with your preschooler are easy trips, slow pace, and flexibility. When your child needs to eat or sleep, don't delay those vital activities. When your young child is ready to go home, pack up. When you are tired or ready to go, it's also okay to head for home. Hint: It's okay to wait until your kids are school age for big adventures. Don't push it too early.

School Age: Balance

School-age children tend to be outgoing and great fun. Your biggest challenge is balancing the goal to teach them with their need to discover the world on their own. Unlike preschoolers, school-age kids can separate reality and fantasy, multitask, and understand more complex topics beyond visual or tactile stimulation. That means you can begin activities that are more complex, longer, and more challenging. School-age kids work well in groups and even become mildly competitive with their peers and them-

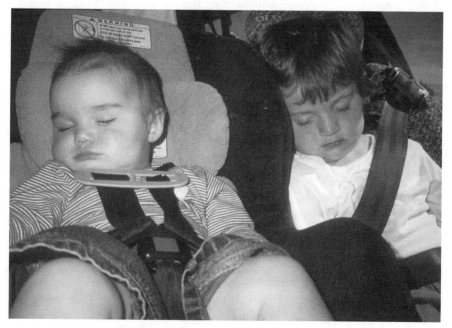

On the way home, plan naps accordingly.

selves. But you have to watch that they don't become too focused on winning and that they learn to be a good sport. They need to follow rules, too, as they may learn to bend them.

School-age kids love adventure but also need friendship and guidance. They need to be challenged a bit, and they love to help with planning, preparation, and decision-making. They may even choose to work on specific skills to better themselves. However, outdoor lessons shouldn't feel like school. Use lots of games with positive feedback, laughs, and rewards. Make new sports fun, or they won't be interested.

A special word of caution: Remember, despite the fact that they are participating in outdoor sports, they are still little people, so they need supervision. Also, kids need to know that their parents are around for help. It's okay to challenge them, if you keep their limitations in mind and watch for warning signs like fatigue, hunger, thirst, or frustration.

There is really no limit to what you can begin to do, especially as school-age kids become physically stronger and their fine motor skills improve. You can ski, snowboard, bike, surf, rock climb, mountaineer, or canoe. The main difference you will find in this age group, especially between five- and ten-year-olds, for example, is the level of activity. My friend Lisa, whose daughters are five and seven, took her kids on a six-week car-camping trip around Oregon. Another friend, Linda, took her three kids, ages eight through twelve, on a month-long hike on the Pacific Crest Trail in Oregon's Cascade Mountains.

The only downside is once your kids are in school, you are somewhat limited to school breaks for extended trips.

Teenagers: Keep It Fun

Teenagers can be pure joy or the most difficult people on the planet. But, as parents of teens know, this is both a wonderful and a challenging age, one with constant trials and joy.

As their cognitive skills rapidly improve, teenagers rely on explanation as well as demonstration. They apply problem-solving and analytical thinking to complex tasks. Parents have the difficult jobs of being coach, mentor, role model, guardian, and peacekeeper all at once. Give positive feedback and constructive criticism, but always treat teens with respect. Be aware of their psyche and spirit, sometimes robust and other times fragile. This can be tricky if the teen is the opposite sex of the parent. Be honest and talk openly, especially about concerns regarding safety. Teens should follow the rules and know that there are consequences if they don't—that can be the hardest job for the parent of a teen.

We throw rocks on a rare clear day in midwinter.

Although teens become stronger, more coordinated, and more skillful, some may have difficulty with the hormonal and physical changes. Some will seemingly adapt to adult bodies overnight and become better athletes than their parents at certain sports. They will want to participate in some activities but not others. Although they want to be independent, they almost always do better with friends. Encourage your teen, but don't force him or her into activities. Some teens adapt quickly to new sports or activities. Others don't take to them right away. Take your time. Pay attention to your children's level of enthusiasm and how they are physically and mentally progressing.

The list of outdoor activities for teenagers is limited only by imagination. You may choose straightforward hikes or bike rides, or you may choose to take your teenagers rafting the Grand Canyon or climbing Mount

Twenty Pearls for Success

Most parents, including me, have asked ourselves at one time or another, "Why am I doing this?" Parenting can be frustrating enough without adding outdoor adventure sports. I don't have a surefire method for success in every circumstance, but I have a number of tips and guidelines that work for my family as well as other outdoor parents and experts. Most topics will be further detailed in later chapters. These may not apply to every family or every situation—remember, every child, family, and adventure will be different.

1. Attitude is everything. Keep a positive attitude, even when things go awry. Kids are very sensitive, and they will know when something is not good. If you teach them to keep spirits positive and work through tough situations, they will carry this lesson with them throughout their lives. It is tough sometimes, especially when you've driven an hour to find clouds pouring rain. Laugh; it helps.
2. Be flexible. Your flexibility will be tested again and again. When you have children, you learn immediately that no matter how much you plan, the unexpected will occur. More than once we packed for a morning hike and drove a half hour to the trailhead only to find both girls asleep in their car seats. I pulled out a book and read while the kids napped.
3. Pay attention to your kids (even teenagers). The cornerstone for safety is supervision. I've said it before, but it's so important. As a doctor, I reinforce this constantly because I see injured kids in the emergency room or at the ski patrol clinic. This doesn't mean you have to be constantly watching your children, but, depending on their age, the activity, your location, and your comfort zone, you should have some level of direct involvement at all times.
4. Have realistic goals. Don't take on a full day for your first outing. Keep things simple at the onset and gradually work up to larger and more complex trips. Have some general age-appropriate goals for your children. Goals should be obtainable and reasonable. However, don't get too caught up in a goal; use it as a general guideline. Remember, the ultimate goal, as far as most kids are concerned, is to have fun.
5. Pay attention to the level of exertion: too much and your child will become tired and prone to injury, too little and he or she will get bored. Kids can get fatigued, physically and mentally.

Plan some downtime or breaks and pay attention to your children. Signs of overstimulation include lack of focus, hyperactivity, poor attention span, and physical fatigue.

6. Teach your children about success and failure. Winning and improving are important but so are putting out 100 percent effort, trying new sports or techniques, spending time with family and friends, and having fun. When asked, older kids respond that they stop sports because they are not having fun or they feel pressure from parents or coaches. This is an important issue. Don't push your kids. If your child wants to stop, find out why and then honor his or her wishes.

7. Give kids some decision-making power. For young kids, this means limited choices and directed decisions. For example: "Do you want to go now or in five minutes?" They should also help with planning and packing, such as making lunch. Older kids should help plan, pack, and unpack.

8. Be prepared for frustration, fear, and embarrassment. Develop good problem-solving skills and alternatives to these emotions when things go wrong. Be supportive, but give your child a chance to deal with tough times. Don't rescue your child from a fearful or embarrassing situation, but help him or her work through it.

9. Check and recheck the weather.

10. Communicate with your kids. With older kids like teenagers, be honest and talk openly about concerns or issues. For younger kids' omnipresent "Why?" answer them directly and truthfully, or perhaps see if they can answer the question themselves. When Skylar asked me why a bird with a broken wing was fluttering I said, "Why do you think?" "Because he has an owie?" she said. Body language is important too. When my oldest daughter tried soccer, I could see she wasn't interested in learning how to kick. She just wanted to run and jump. So, we enrolled her in gymnastics camp instead, and she loved it.

11. Remind kids to say please and thank you. Kids should take turns, wait for the group, and help others in need. Don't let your kids slide by with poor manners that they wouldn't get away with at home. Teach cooperation and responsibility. It will pay off in the long run.

Continued on next page

12. Prepare as much as possible ahead of time, especially food and drinks. When we go skiing, we try to pack the night before (the kids help too). We have a gigantic duffel bag for both daughters' ski gear. In the morning, we get completely dressed and put on sunscreen at home. That way we have less to do when we get to the mountain.

13. Get the best equipment you can afford. I'll discuss gear in subsequent chapters.

14. Try to keep some semblance of routine. You don't need a rigid schedule. Part of the fun of outdoor adventure is getting out of the mold of everyday life, but at the same time, kids like routine. They like to know they will get snacks and lunch on time, and rest time is an important part of kids' days. When my kids were young, a morning activity, such as skiing or a bike ride, was followed by lunch; then we were in the car driving home during naptime, and the kids usually zonked out immediately.

15. Take breaks for water and snacks. Just like us, kids get grumpy and irritable if they don't get enough food or fluids. Unlike adults, kids often don't know that the problem is hunger or thirst. When out and about, take plenty of snacks and water. Stop and eat every two hours, and have drinks available every thirty minutes. Special treats are handy too (it's okay to give your child M&Ms once in a while).

16. Bring Band-Aids (actually, a complete first aid kit). On a trip to Mexico, my daughter asked for Winnie-the-Pooh Band-Aids every time she got a boo-boo. It wasn't that she was bleeding every time, but this was her way of getting comfort when she got hurt. This was especially important since we were away from home for two weeks and in a foreign country. Be prepared for injury; it will occur to every child sooner or later.

17. Bring some comfort from home, like a stuffed animal or favorite game, especially for longer trips. When we travel, we bring my daughters' favorite pillowcases. They are easy to pack, and wherever we sleep, the kids feel like they are sleeping in their own beds.

18. Get help. Ask for help from grandma and grandpa (they can go along or watch the kids for an afternoon while you pack for vacation). Set your teenager loose on the internet to research a

particular place or activity. Guidebooks are a wonderful source of information, especially those geared toward families with children. Use them to find good hikes or bike trails as well as specific information for the area you want to visit. If you are going to a national park, forest, or wilderness area, check with rangers. Ask your friends, who may have good ideas on where to go. From friends, we got a hot tip to visit the Oregon Coast Aquarium while on a trip to the beach. My kids absolutely loved it. They peered into the shark pool, watched otters frolic, and touched starfish and sea anemones in the touch pool.

19. Don't be afraid to stop, especially while you are still having fun. We hear "Just five more minutes" from our kids nearly every time we get ready to leave the swimming pool. However, if we leave with my daughters still wanting to swim, they will be enthusiastic to come again, and we don't risk injury by continuing when they are fatigued. With older kids, you may have to peel them away from the campground at the lake. After they meet new friends, they might want to stay all summer.

20. Bring along friends and their families. Most kids love having their friends along. Often it makes life easier and more fun for parents, since it gives us a chance to trade off with supervisory activities.

And one more tip: stay home. Most parents, myself included, have learned this lesson the hard way. You had planned a camping trip to the beach weeks in advance and you packed two days before. But when you woke, your child had a runny nose and a cough. The plans go down the tubes, and you stay home all day. If you try to force a trip that your child is not physically or mentally ready for, no one will have fun. It's okay to cancel a trip.

Remember, every once in a while things go awry for no obvious reason. That's part of the challenge of being a parent. The weather's a little cool, your child didn't sleep well the night before, or you left the favorite stuffed animal at home. Once, I ran with the Baby Jogger, with my two daughters riding in it, through the wooded trail to the library. We had snacks, we had water, and we had a good night's sleep. Nonetheless, when we arrived at the library my oldest said she wanted to go home and started crying. We went home and had a great morning doing puzzles on the kitchen table. Go figure.

Rainier. It is very important for your teenager to be involved with the entire trip, including planning, decision-making, and unpacking. Hint: They can help with the dirty laundry and dishes too. Pick an activity they are interested in, perhaps something they suggest. Above all, keep it fun.

PARENTS CAN HAVE FUN TOO

You have now read about the benefits of outdoor adventure sports—psychological, educational, and physical—as well as guidelines for the different age groups of children. Your role in a nutshell is to go with your kids and help them along the way. Get them psyched about your passion, whatever the sport or activity. If they want to do a sport that you haven't tried, learn it with them. That can be a blast for parents and kids alike.

When they are younger, you'll need to supervise everything: lunch, clothing, equipment, and safety gear. You will need to make what-when-where final decisions. As they grow into adulthood, your relationship will change into one of shared tasks and mutual decisions. The ever-changing relationships with your children are one of the deep pleasures of parenthood. It is important that you recognize changes in the relationships and alter your approach accordingly.

In this book I won't talk much about success, because any time you head outside you are successful, even if you drive to the park and then turn around and drive home because big black clouds are pouring buckets of rain. Everywhere in our culture kids are pressured to succeed: in school, on the playground, at home. It is good to set goals when you are outside playing, but consider other parameters like having a safe trip and keeping it fun. For example, with young kids, don't set goals like ten ski runs or hiking to the summit of a peak—you'll miss the experience along the way and risk becoming overwhelmed by a goal. Older kids do want to reach the summit of a mountain or the end of the trail, but if the goal is not reached, the trip should still be a success. Goals are good; just set reasonable ones consistent with the age and ability of your children, and don't focus too much on them. Your goals will change as your family grows and develops.

Also, you don't have to travel to exotic locations to take advantage of the outdoors. Use your imagination and stay within your budget. Good spots for adventure are often close-by. Keep it simple, and you will head out more often. You can walk, hike, baby jog, or bike in most city parks. Within an hour or two of your home, you can probably find a state park, nature preserve, or recreation area. Snow skiing is located within an hour or two of many urban areas across the U.S. If you don't ski or snowboard, try sledding, snowshoeing, or playing in the snow. Remember, keep it simple from the start and gradually work up to longer and more complex outings.

It does take energy, effort, and time to take your kids on outdoor adventures. But the rewards are huge and adventures become much easier as your children get older. Knowing how to get started is perhaps the largest barrier to adventure sports. This book is designed to help you explore adventure sports step by step. I simplified the process, using my own experiences as well as those from many other outdoor experts who are also parents. And I've kept it fun.

Finally, parents ought to have fun, too, and gain something personally from every adventure. I'm giving you permission, in some way, however minuscule, to be a bit self-centered. With young children, your primary goal and satisfaction may be from participating in your child's life and spending quality time with your family. But later, you may have some personal goals like reaching the summit of a peak, hiking to a new waterfall, or making ten laps around the park instead of nine. It is not only okay for parents to gain some level of personal satisfaction from achievement, it is important for us to have fun too.

2

Ready, Set, Go:
Planning and Packing

Planning and packing should be part of the fun for everyone. Try to view this not as a chore but as part of the fun. Involve your kids. They will learn the importance of proper preparation and make the process more fun. My daughters love packing their clothes the night before and assembling their activities for the car, such as books, art pencils and paper, and toys. I also have them help me with grocery shopping. That way they can't complain as much if they don't like a certain food. In this chapter, I'll discuss the nuts and bolts of packing, namely food, drink, and clothing requirements and some general tips on packing and planning.

FOOD FOR ADVENTURE

Food can be the simplest thing to pack for older kids or fairly complex, if you have picky eaters. Meals may require the finely tuned art of coaching, or rather, pleading. Like all parents, I initially worried that my first child was not getting enough to eat because she was such a picky eater when she was young. There are lots of books on nutrition and food for children. Much of the advice, when applied to outdoor trips, can be distilled to a few simple concepts.

For adventures, keep food simple, nutritious, and healthy. Make sure you have several items that your child likes. Peanut butter sandwiches are a quick, easy, and healthy favorite for all ages. Cheese is a good source of protein. Milk is loaded with calories; it is really more of a food than a drink since it contains lots of quality protein and fat. Apples, carrots, bananas, crackers, trail mix, and granola bars all make great adventure foods. Traveling is probably not the best time to try a new food, unless you feel doubly adventurous. Also, bring foods that require little or no preparation.

Pack plenty of food for everyone. Sometimes mom and dad are so busy

A kid's camera makes a great outdoor activity.

they forget to pack adult food. Once, I took my young kids to the wildlife refuge for a picnic, and I unloaded a feast of kid's food: fish crackers, peeled apple slices, cheese squares, raisins, and peanut butter crackers. Needless to say, I had packed nothing for myself, so I had to eat leftover kid's food.

It is okay to bring a treat, as long as it is limited in quantity and healthy. We usually bring some homemade cookies. We almost always have some emergency chocolate candy like M&Ms for times when we need a lift: a sudden rainstorm when everyone gets cold and wet or when everyone is tired and we still have another twenty minutes to get back to the car. Remember, candy is not universally bad, nor is it completely unhealthy. Just keep quantities small and limited to special occasions. Once, on a stormy ride up the chairlift at our local ski area, I pulled out some Cheerios for snacks. My daughter informed me, "These are not the right kind of treats, Papa. Mommy brings Smarties," referring to the tiny sugar candies. "It's okay," I said. "These are Papa snacks." Luckily that worked.

Try to keep your eating times roughly the same as when you are at home. But stay flexible. If you just finished lunch and your child says, "I'm still hungry," feed him or her. When you are participating in a hike or bike

*Never forget food:
A big family needs a
big lunch.*

ride, it is not necessarily the best time to teach hungry children that they should have eaten all their lunch. When on outdoor adventures, it is most important that children eat, and less so what, when, and how much. Adults tend to eat on a schedule or when we are hungry. Kids don't often pay attention to the time of day or the hunger pang. A good rule is to have a meal or a snack every two hours. Stop before your kids get hungry or thirsty.

FLUIDS FOR ADVENTURE
Water is life's sustenance; we all know that. You should never go on an outdoor trip without a water bottle or hydration bladder backpack. Keep water handy at all times so your kids can drink often when on an adventure. Pay attention to how much your child drinks. Constant intake of fluids, even small amounts, is important, especially in cold or hot weather, when more water is required. As with eating, sometimes kids tend to forget to drink water, and often they don't realize when they are thirsty. I remember once

taking my daughter to the park when she had just started walking. She became cranky and irritable, but I just couldn't figure out what was wrong. Finally, when she saw the water bottle, she pointed and let out a large scream. She drank her entire bottle. Instantly she was back to her normal temperament. Neither she nor I realized she needed water.

Make your kids take a drink when you prepare to leave your car, take water breaks regularly, and drink some when you finish your trip. A good rule is to stop for a water break every twenty to thirty minutes or so. In warm weather, you may need to stop more often.

The amount of water your children should drink is not exactly scientific. They should be constantly drinking throughout a day of activity. Adults need a gallon of water per day with strenuous physical activity in a warm climate. For kids, water requirements depend on factors such as activity level, ambient temperature, direct sun, elevation, how much they sweat, and other factors. The single best gauge is to watch their urine. If they go to the bathroom every hour or two and their urine is light yellow or clear, then they are getting enough water. If they don't urinate much and it is concentrated or dark yellow, they need to drink more. Remember, thirst is a late sign, especially for little guys. They won't say "I'm thirsty" until they are dehydrated.

Start out right with a big breakfast.

Stay hydrated during a midsummer campout.

Some debate exists as to just what to drink. For most kids, water or water mixed with juice is best for hydration. Actually, full-strength juice is probably just fine for most situations. Some parents feel it has too much sugar, but when kids are outside, they can usually use the extra energy.

Gatorade, Tang, Kool-Aid, or other sweetened drinks for kids are okay, although I usually don't bring them for our family. They work well to hydrate kids, but most brands have lots of sugar. The basic benefits of sports or sugar drinks are that they replace some electrolytes like sodium and potassium, they have sugar for quick energy, and they may be absorbed quicker than water. The first point is especially important when adults sweat, because they lose electrolytes. However, with kids who drink often and eat snacks, this is less of an issue. I generally offer my kids sweetened drinks only on special occasions. If you give your child sweetened drinks, dilute them to half strength with water.

It's okay for kids to drink milk, but since it has so much fat and protein, it's not the best choice if you are trying to keep an active child hydrated. If your child will drink nothing but milk, that's probably okay for mild activity in mild weather. But for long hikes or bike rides, especially in hot weather, you should make a point of getting your child to drink water, juice,

Procuring Water

If you need to obtain water in the wilderness, you should be careful. Springs are usually pure, but running or standing water is often tainted with microorganisms that can cause illness. A common parasite called *Giardia* is prevalent in many mountain streams in America. It causes diarrhea and makes kids susceptible to dehydration. Rodents and other critters transmit *Giardia,* so it can be anywhere.

For extended trips or emergencies, you should be prepared to purify water. The easiest method is to use a chemical treatment such as iodine tablets. You can buy these at any outdoor store. One or two tablets in a bottle of water will purify it in an hour. The water tastes terrible, so you can buy an additional tablet that neutralizes the chemical and removes the taste. You should know that too much of these chemicals can be bad for you or your child. It's best to save this for emergencies. I always carry a small bottle of iodine tablets in my survival or first aid kit, but I've rarely needed them.

A newer technology is the MSR/MIOX system. This small purifier is the size of a penlight. You add a teaspoon of salt and a tablespoon of water. Press a button and a battery-powered electric current creates an antioxidant solution. This can be added to a quart of water to kill dangerous microorganisms.

Another time-tested method is a mechanical hand pump. Outdoor pumps are available from outdoor stores and can be carried in your car or backpack. The most basic pumps are filters. These have ceramic, paper, or composite filters that remove parasites as well as most bacteria. Viruses, on the other hand, are too small to be filtered. A better option for a hand pump is a purifier. These work the same as filters, but they have a chemical impregnated in the cartridge. In addition to filtering parasites and bacteria, viruses are killed by the chemical. Some have a third function: After chemical neutralization, water passes through a charcoal filter that removes the chemical to improve taste. Be advised, like any piece of equipment, hand pumps require cleaning and replacement of cartridges after extended use. With care, they last a long time.

A third option is boiling water. This takes time as well as a camp stove and fuel, which can be heavy for a day outing. If you are car camping and are preparing a meal, this is perhaps an easy option.

or a flavored water-based drink. Keep trying, and soon you'll find a brand of juice or drink they like.

If you have little kids, remember to bring a spill-proof cup or water bottle with a lid so they don't get their clothes or backpacks wet. For older kids, a standard water bottle with a spout that closes works fine. When traveling, my friend Jon brings his CamelBak for his family. It is a water bladder with a drinking tube that looks like a gigantic straw, perfect for the small mouth of his son.

If you run out of water or if you are on a long hike or camping trip, you may need to get water from a stream or lake. Procuring water is an important issue in outdoor adventure. In general, mountain and forest streams are not safe to drink from in the United States. Many have *Giardia,* a small protozoan that causes diarrhea. Other streams have bacterial and viral critters from cattle, wild animals, or human waste. Similarly, when traveling abroad, especially to developing countries, microorganisms may contaminate water. For purifying water, there are three chief methods: mechanical pumping, boiling, or chemical treatment.

WILD KIDS' FASHION

Clothing is actually important equipment. You need to protect your child from the natural elements, but you don't want to break the bank. Kids' clothes can be dirt cheap or ridiculously expensive. Fortunately, outdoor clothes are durable. You can often use hand-me-downs or borrow from friends. Try to find deals: For example, winter clothes go on sale after Christmas. Internet or mail-order catalogs sometimes offer better prices, if you know exactly what you're looking for and you are not picky about color or style. Also, for some clothing, you can buy one or two sizes larger and roll up sleeves or pant cuffs, or tuck pants into boots. This works great for ski pants or rain gear. Then you may be able to get more than one season from a jacket or pants. Buy unisex styles and colors so boys and girls can pass them to other siblings, relatives, or friends.

Bright-colored clothing is fun for kids. It also serves another function— it is visible in foul weather or thick woods. Yellow, orange, pink, and white are the most visible colors in the wilderness. Red tends to look brown at dawn or dusk. Coats with reflector tape, strips, piping, or patches are great. These light up brightly in car headlights or flashlight beams to provide added visibility and an extra margin of safety.

Also, consider dressing your children alike. It is much easier to keep track of them if you are in a busy place. When I was seven, we took a family trip to Disneyland, and every day my mom dressed my brother, sister, and me in matching pants and shirts. I felt ridiculous being dressed like my two siblings, but three decades and two daughters later, I now realize the vital importance of making it as easy as possible to keep track of the kids, especially at a busy place like a ski resort cafeteria or an airport in Mexico.

Kids need one of four types of clothing for different types of weather and activity: sun, rain, cold, and water. Fortunately, you probably have much of this clothing already.

Sun Clothing

Wilderness medicine experts report that one sunburn in childhood poses an increased risk for skin cancer later in life. Sun-protective clothing should be worn in addition to sunscreen for a number of reasons. Clothing is a protective barrier that stays on, whereas sunscreen can wear off with sweat, water, or time. And sometimes it is difficult to cover the entire exposed skin with sunscreen. Actually, many parents don't put enough sunscreen on their

Sunscreen

It is important to use sunscreen in conjunction with sun-protective clothing. Sunscreen needs to be put on thick and often—it wears off with sweat and water during the day. Sometimes it is difficult to get all your child's exposed skin covered, especially ears and face and behind the neck. Sunscreen designed for children is hypoallergenic and gentle on the skin. It should be rated to 25 SPF (Sun Protection Factor) or greater. Make sure you use a golf-ball-size blob on a fifty-pound kid. Cover all exposed skin, especially face, neck, arms, and legs.

In general, the more difficult it is to put on, the better it works. Spray-on sunscreen wears off quickly, but the heavy, thick, creamy waterproof sunscreen, applied properly, lasts much longer.

I've found it can be difficult to get my child to cooperate when applying the lotion. On a trip to Baja, I tried to put sunscreen on my three-year-old daughter every morning. Despite my varying tactics—coaxing, insistence, and threats—she acted like it was battery acid when it touched her skin; she screamed and yelled when I gently applied it. Finally, I sat her down and told her that she needed to wear it because the sun can cause owies on her skin. That worked.

kids. The general recommendation is a gram of sunscreen per square inch of skin, double what most people actually use. This means you should use a golf-ball-size blob of sunscreen to cover the body of a fifty-pound child.

Loose-fitting, light-colored cotton clothing works best for sun protection. Long pants and long sleeves are recommended. Before we went on a trip to Baja, I bought several inexpensive long-sleeved white shirts for my toddler and long-sleeved white onesies for my infant at an outlet store. These clothes were their sun staples for two weeks. A sun hat with a wide brim and chin strap and glasses will protect a child's head and face. Buy a colorful sun hat, or better, let your child pick one out. Washable, crushable sun hats in light colors work best. The real trick is keeping the clothes and hat on during sun play or activities.

Considering the damaging rays of the sun, many parents ask me if it's okay to let their kids run naked on the beach. If you've ever seen your kids do this, you'll know how fun it can be. It is okay as long as it is appropriate with your surrounding company. Make sure you put on plenty of sunscreen, limit the nakedness to fifteen minutes, and avoid the most direct sun from 10 A.M. to 2 P.M.

Rain Clothing

Rain clothes are much easier to get a child to wear because kids don't like to get wet. Get a good rain suit, but don't spend a bundle. Gore-Tex or other expensive, high-tech fabrics usually aren't necessary for young kids. Many of those fabrics are designed to keep one dry from rain as well as to allow sweat to evaporate. Young kids don't sweat much, so they don't necessarily need the features of those fabrics. And they certainly don't need all the fancy pockets, double front zippers, or armpit zippers. Plus, they will grow out of their clothes quickly. Rubberized nylon keeps kids dry and warm. It's inexpensive and durable.

I have found that some additional features are important. A hood is useful when you forget or lose a hat (not if, but when). Cuffs with snaps and elastic are great, especially when you buy clothes one size larger. The snap and elastic cuffs keep the rain suit from falling down and keeps pants tight on boots for tramping in puddles.

We always carry rubber boots, mandatory for splashing in puddles. Your children will grow out of them long before the boots wear out, so get something basic and inexpensive. Don't buy them too big, or your kid will trip when running. We tend to make a special deal out of boots so our kids will like wearing them. Skylar's are red with spider designs on the top. Avrie's are bright yellow with pink stripes. Try putting stickers on the boots too. Teenagers might prefer to use lightweight hiking boots, which are more comfortable and not as hot. They are not totally waterproof, so teens should bring a spare pair of dry socks.

I'm not a big fan of umbrellas. First, I grew up in the Pacific Northwest, where we use jackets with hoods. Second, umbrellas are just extra gear that your kid will play with more than use to keep dry. Third, they have the disadvantage of being slightly dangerous, because the knobs on the ribs can poke someone in the face or eye.

Warm Clothing for Cool Weather

Warm clothes are essential for most kids in almost any climate. You definitely don't need to get name-brand fleece or long underwear. Stick with basic colors and unisex styles. Always bring extra wherever you travel, especially if you are going to the mountains or if you will be splashing in puddles. Be advised: fleece, polypropylene, and other synthetic fabrics are flammable. Be cautious and attentive when sitting around a campfire. Alternatively, kids should wear cotton or wool clothing, which are less flammable near a fire.

Usually, warm clothing comes in three layers: a next-to-skin base layer, a middle insulating layer (or two), and an outer wind- and waterproof shell. Long underwear is a good base layer. It should be made from polypropylene, which is warm and withstands multiple washings. It also makes great backup pajamas if you are tight on space in your suitcase.

For middle insulating layers, I like washable fleece. Polyester fleece pants and shirts are our staples; fleece is warm even when wet, quick to dry, and washable. It is also inexpensive.

For outerwear, you will need a coat and pants that are made of tightly woven nylon with some sort of insulating material. Make sure they are washable. Coats that are heavily insulated are nice because you don't have to stack layers of sweaters on your child. When you go in for hot chocolate, it's nice for kids to be able to take off their coats and not have multiple layers of sweaters to take off. Choose down or bulky synthetic insulation if you spend a lot of time in colder climates. Fleece insulation is usually not as warm but is more versatile and easier to wash.

I like full zippered jackets with hoods for our kids; jackets are much easier to put on and take off than pullovers, and a hood is handy when you can't find a hat. Pullovers work fine too and may be better if you kid likes to take his or her clothes off (they are more difficult for parents to get on and off too). I like pants instead of bib overalls. Although they provide some extra warmth for the trunk and hold a shirt tucked in, they are more difficult for kids to pull down to go to the bathroom.

Warm boots are very important too. For the occasional trip to the mountains, your child can wear double socks with his or her rain boots. But generally, for regular trips to the snow, your kid will need winter boots. Look for those that zip or Velcro, as they will be easier for your child to remove when going in the house. It's okay to buy them a bit big, and that way you might get two or three seasons' use before your kid grows out of them.

Don't forget accessories. A hat is mandatory for warmth. Mittens are much warmer than gloves. Retainer clips are essential to keep mittens attached to coats for younger kids; otherwise you'll lose the mittens the first time your child takes them off (which is usually in the first five minutes of wearing them). For socks, wool-nylon blends are perhaps the warmest and most durable. Always bring extra socks if you plan on splashing in puddles or playing in the snow. Don't spend a bundle on accessories. We have a dozen single socks and single mittens in our ski bag (the mates tend to disappear).

Water Clothing

Water clothes vary widely depending on the type of activity. A swimsuit is okay for pools, but it usually doesn't offer much sun protection or warmth. The new standard swimsuit in Australia is a T-shirt and shorts made from Lycra or another synthetic material. This style provides more coverage for sun protection. Additionally, the shirt and shorts are warm.

Another option when swimming in cool water or direct sun is a polypropylene long underwear top. You may have one in your cold weather gear already. Polypropylene is inexpensive, warm when wet, and quick to dry. This is a great option for snorkeling or a day at the lake, if you don't have a sun top for your child. See chapter 10 for wetsuits, specific for cold water sports.

Now all this clothing is great, but you are probably wondering, "How do I keep my grade-school kids from taking everything off, or how do I convince them to wear a hat and mittens?" This can be the most difficult part of an adventure. Here are some hints.

- Explain to kids why they need to wear clothes, whether it is a hat, mittens, or rain boots.
- Offer a reward or treat if they keep their clothes on. This doesn't have to be candy or a new toy; it can be a sticker, a hug, or a high-five.
- Allow your kids to experience the elements briefly without warm clothes or rain gear. At home, let your child run in the rain without his or her raincoat or boots. Kids learn quickly that they don't like to be cold and wet.

- Try to get friends to wear the same level of protection, especially if their friends are older. It is much easier to get your child to wear a sun hat in summer or mittens in winter if friends or older kids do the same.
- Sometimes, for whatever reason, my oldest daughter won't wear the pink mittens, but she will wear the purple ones. This is a battle I choose not to fight.

ESSENTIAL EQUIPMENT

Without our tools and accessories, heading outdoors is nearly impossible. Luckily, gear for outdoor kids is well designed, durable, and readily available. It can be expensive, though, so you will have to weigh the durability and accessories of more costly equipment with the scaled-down versions of cheaper gear. You are balancing price with quality and features; somewhere you will find a happy middle ground that works for your family.

Sport-specific equipment is discussed in part 2, but the general essentials are discussed here. When shopping, it always helps if you can rent or borrow more expensive gear first. That way you can see if you like it before you spend the money.

Day Pack

For almost all kids, you will need a basic day pack. This inexpensive backpack will hold your essentials. Over-the-shoulder diaper bags don't work as well because often you need both hands free or you may need to carry the bag for several hours.

Pack a water bottle and snacks no matter where and when you go. For younger kids, it's nice to have a change of clothes and basic accessories, depending on the season. For example, we always carry a sun hat and a small tube of sunscreen in the summer. In winter, we have a warm hat and gloves in the bag for both kids.

Younger kids can carry their own small backpacks with food, a water bottle, and perhaps a small toy or book. Keep it light, since you may end up stuffing it in your bag. Older kids will pack what they think they need. However, you might take a peek in their bags just before leaving the house to make sure they've packed the essentials.

For long trips in a car, plane, train, or boat, you may need toys or entertainment. Keep toys, games, or activities to a minimum, just what can fit in your bag. For younger kids, bring crayons and a color book, reading books, art pencils and paper, and a favorite stuffed animal or doll. Tapes or CDs are great fun too. Because my kids are younger, their favorite car toys are

The art kit is always good for some quiet-time activities.

magnetic drawing boards, travel puzzles, and an art kit with colored pens and pencils. It helps to have toys for car trips that your kids don't normally play with; that way your kids won't get bored with them as quickly. For long trips, videos may be appropriate if your vehicle has a portable television (some minivans have televisions built in). I tend to think my kids watch enough TV at home, so we don't have one.

Older kids will want to bring books, magazines, or electronics such as a personal CD or MP3 player, a PDA, or a hand-held computer game. If your child brings such electronics, bring backup batteries. They'll owe you one. Alternatively, get an adapter for the power point in your car.

My kids love music for the car ride. We know the entire soundtrack from *The Sound of Music* by heart and have listened to Disney's *60 Years of Music* about a thousand times. Sometimes you can find something everyone likes. When traveling with grandma and grandpa, we listen to the soundtrack from *Seven Brides for Seven Brothers* or, more recently, They Might Be

How Kids Can Help

Kids can do lots for planning and preparation; in fact, that's part of the fun of organizing a trip, and that's how they learn. You're probably thinking you can do everything yourself in half the time. But spend the additional time to let your kids help. Remember, the whole point is for them to learn and participate in the adventure, even if it does take more time. It's the process as much as the activity that is so important. When they get older, it will be old habit for them to participate in the planning, packing, and cleanup. Here are some ideas.

- Let your children help you pick out snacks and pack lunch.
- Show them on the map where you are going. Discuss how long it will take to get there.
- Discuss what clothes are needed, and let your children help pick them out. For example, if you are going skiing, go through the list of mittens, hats, helmets, long underwear, ski parkas and pants, and accessories.
- Help them pick out a few activities for the car.
- Let them pack their bags. Even school-age kids can carry a small backpack with a snack and a light coat (be prepared for them to get tired of carrying it). Check younger kids' bags to make sure something vital isn't left behind.
- It is important when you get home that they help you unpack. This is easier for older kids. You will need help unloading the car, drying and washing clothes, unpacking the lunch box, and cleaning up. It's crucial for kids to unpack, to help make trips less burdensome for parents and to teach children that the trip is not finished until unpacking and cleaning are done.

Giants' *NO!* album. We take turns picking music, and sometimes my kids have to listen to my wife's or my CDs.

For any car trip, keep snacks and water bottles handy. As soon as you pull out of the driveway you may hear, "I'm hungry," from the backseat. Don't endanger your family by looking for a water bottle or snack bag buried deep in an inaccessible backpack. Take a potty break before and after any car ride. More than once we've left the park only to stop three minutes later when someone from the backseat yelled, "I gotta go potty!"

Travel Games

I spy: Take turns guessing objects.

Twenty questions: One has twenty questions to find an object.

Tic-tac-toe: Draw two sets of perpendicular lines, then alternate X and O to get three in a row.

Ghost: Take turns calling out a letter. Try not to spell a word but get the other person to complete one.

Alphabet game: Try to find letters in sequence on billboards or signs.

Buzz: Try not to say the number 7 when counting in sequence.

Animal questions: "If you were an alligator, where would you live?"

License plate: Watch for certain states or specific numbers and letters.

Safety Gear

Most kids can't carry a lot of survival or safety equipment. Usually, if they have a small backpack, it will be full of snacks, water, and a book or stuffed animal. If you want them to carry an additional safety item, give them a whistle. First, send them into the backyard to blow their hearts out. Once the novelty wears off, teach them to blow it only if they are in trouble or if they get separated from you. We have whistles attached to my daughters' ski coats for such emergencies.

It's also nice for older kids to carry a light, such as a pocket flashlight or a small headlamp. This helps if they get lost at night. They can use it to signal or to find their way down the trail. Older kids might also enjoy carrying a map and compass and a first aid kid designed for kids, and they will become familiar with these safety items. You can even spend some time before you go or during downtime on your trip explaining how to use them.

Most kids can be trusted with a hand-held radio. This is great if you get separated or you choose to let your teenagers hike ahead on the trail or ski by themselves. Radios are great for safety and fun. These Family Radio Station (FRS) radios are common on hikes or at ski resorts now. Sometimes park rangers or ski patrollers monitor emergency channels. Usually this is channel 9, security code 11. A cell phone is another option, but you may not always get reception.

You should also bring a complete first aid kit. See chapters 17 and 18 for more information on first aid and survival kits.

Duffel Bags: One for Every Season
In addition to our day pack, duffels bags are the mainstay for packing my family's other gear, especially clothing. For example, we have one for ski clothes, another for swim wear, and a third for rain gear. We have a mesh bag to hold all the soccer balls and cones, a second for beach toys, and a third for bike helmets, pads, and gloves. This makes it simple, easy, and quick when heading out for a day of adventure. We can grab the right bag, throw a few extra things in, and away we go. Typically, one bag tends to stay in the car for months at time, depending on the season.

When we return from an adventure, we wash the clothes or dry the wet items and then repack the bag so it is ready for the next trip. At the end of the season, we clean and pack everything neatly so it's ready for the next year.

Well before the season, unpack the bag, try on the clothes, and make sure things fit. Try on ski and snowboard clothing in August so you can look for deals in September and October for items your kids grew out of. Also, try on bike helmets well before the first days of spring.

YOUR VEHICLE
Your vehicle will be your sanctuary for many trips, especially for day trips close to home. A minivan or sport utility vehicle is perhaps the best all-around vehicle for stuffing in bags of gear and clothing as well as kids. But you don't need to buy a new car. Plenty of adventure can be had in your station wagon or mid-size family car. Our ten-year-old charcoal gray Suburban, dubbed the Gorilla by grandma, is our portable home when on the road.

Car Seats
Car seats are mandatory. All kids under age thirteen should be in the back-seat of your car and in a car seat until they reach age eight or eighty pounds. These new federal guidelines are more strict, and safer, than the previous guidelines. They were enacted because seatbelts don't fit children well. However, in some states the law is still age six or sixty pounds. Some newer cars have special straps or adjusters for younger kids. In general, your car seat will be one of three models: infant, convertible, or booster.

1. A rear-facing infant seat is used from birth until your child reaches twenty pounds or twenty-seven inches. Your child's head should be at least two inches below the top of the seat.

2. Convertible seats are the most versatile. Depending on the brand and model, these seats can be used from twenty up to sixty pounds. Most convertible seats come with a tether that can be used when the seat is facing forward. The tether gives the seat another attachment in addition to the seatbelt; this adds a large margin of safety.

3. Once your child outgrows a convertible seat, a booster is required in most states until he or she is above sixty or eighty pounds. The shoulder belt should come across the collarbone and chest; the lap belt should be snug on the hips.

Except for boosters, child safety seats come with either three- or five-point restraining harnesses. Make sure the straps fit well and are adjustable. For rear-facing seats, straps should be at or below the shoulders. For forward-facing ones, they should be aligned with or slightly above your child's shoulders. The straps should be tight enough so that you can only pass two fingers between the straps and your child's chest. Most harnesses come with a retainer clip to hold the straps together at the chest; this should be at armpit level. Take time to adjust the straps. If your child is bundled up in snow clothes, straps can be too tight; if he or she sheds clothing on the way home, they can be too loose.

Always bring extra socks and shoes when kids will be splashing in water.

Don't Forget!

- Winter or sun hat
- Sunscreen
- Coat
- Extra clothing
- Snacks and lunch

- Water bottle
- Activities for the car ride
- First aid kit and basic survival gear

Car seats make great highchairs for meals too. We lugged our two car seats all the way to Mexico, using them in the airplane and in the taxi getting to and from our beach house at the beginning and end of our trip. But we used them daily for two weeks as highchairs since there were none at the cabana where we stayed.

Hauling Your Gear

Make sure all your gear is either in the trunk, in the cargo bay, or attached properly to the roof. If you need to swerve or stop quickly, the last thing you need is a snowboard or soccer ball shooting to the front of your vehicle.

If you tie gear on the roof, use the appropriate sport rack and attachment. Most sport racks have attachment accessories for bikes, kayaks, surfboards, and rooftop boxes. Rooftop cargo boxes are an excellent way to stash gear on the roof. These lightweight boxes are lockable and waterproof. They come in several sizes and can hold skis and snowboards, camping gear, and luggage. When we go camping, our rooftop box holds two tents, sleeping bags, pads, chairs, blankets, soccer balls, beach toys, and bike helmets.

Another great option for bikes, especially if you have small kids, is a hitch-mounted bike rack. These extend from your car's trailer hitch and hold two or four bikes behind the vehicle. They are great for kids' bikes for two reasons. First, they hold all shapes and sizes of bikes; small kids' bikes usually don't fit well on rooftop racks. Second, when your child grows into a larger bike, you can use the same rack.

That's your primer for planning and packing the essentials: food, water, clothing, and equipment. Don't worry, you will forget something. But that's okay. You and your kids will learn to improvise. Remember, get the best gear you can afford, but don't break the bank. And you will learn as you go. The more trips, the better you will understand your family's food, water, and clothing requirements.

Special Issues for Infants and Toddlers

Many people ask me how old their kids should be before they start adventuring outside. Lots of outdoor enthusiasts want to get outside with their kids when they are still under one year old. But parents worry, and rightfully so, about cold weather, sun exposure, and other hazards. It is okay to head into the outdoors with young kids; in fact, it's preferable to get started early. It takes additional time and energy on your part to head out with infants and toddlers, but it can also be easier. Food is simple if they are breast- or bottle-feeding, and you don't necessarily need to worry about potty breaks if they are still in diapers.

Rest assured that adventures will be fun and rewarding for you as a parent. And the more you go, the easier it gets. Perhaps most important, you will be laying the groundwork for your kids to have a lifelong enthusiasm for the outdoors.

Try something simple like a hike or baby jog. Not only will short trips outdoors give you some healthy alternatives to regular day-to-day activities, your kids will have a blast. My kids started doing outdoor activities before they could walk. They loved having the wind in their faces when they were little. Now, camping, biking, hiking, and skiing are regular activities we do as a family.

When to start? A good time for basic trips is when your child is old enough to hold up his or her head. If you head outdoors with your infants, you will be carrying them in a running stroller, a child-carry backpack, or a frontpack. Thus they need to be able to support their heads on their own. Generally, this means they should be between six and nine months old. Some kids can support their heads earlier, and some later. If you are questioning it, ask your doctor if your child is ready for the running stroller or backpack.

Start early; take the little one hiking.

My wife and I took our oldest child, Skylar, out hiking when she was six months old. We started out quite simple. Our first adventure was a two-hour hike up a popular trail in the Columbia Gorge National Scenic Area near our home. We picked a warm sunny day with a clear blue sky. Timing is very important. I packed food and clothing in the morning. We waited to leave so we could make the thirty-minute drive during Skylar's morning nap. She slept during the drive and at the parking lot while I got all the hiking stuff ready: child-carry backpack, diapers, wet wipes, extra clothes, hat, warm coat, snacks, water, and the musical stuffed Pooh doll. When Skylar woke, we took plenty of time to change her diaper and give her a snack in the car. Then we set off with Skylar in the child-carry backpack.

We didn't make it very far. About thirty minutes and one mile later, we stopped along the river in the sun to have a snack and point out birds and the rushing water. After another half hour of hiking, Skylar wanted to get out of the backpack again. We found a warm spot in the sun where my wife could breast-feed my daughter. When we had enough for our first adventure, we headed down the trail. On our way back, Skylar started crying for no particular reason. The only thing that soothed her was my voice singing, or rather yelling, "Ants Go Marching." We sang it all the way down the trail. Skylar had a big smile on her face when we got back to the car.

She had so much fun on hikes that later that winter, just before her first birthday, we took her skiing in the child-carry backpack too.

GEARING UP

Here are a few basic pointers for what to take with your young children into the outdoors.

Mini Diaper Bag

You probably have a gigantic diaper bag for your young children, but it is often not practical to take a huge bag on a hike or baby jog. You won't have much room in the child-carry backpack or running stroller. When my kids were young I assembled several mini diaper bags. In a one-gallon resealable freezer bag I put a travel container of wet wipes, a diaper or two, a spare plastic bag for wet or dirty diapers, and a small twelve-inch changing pad. Sometimes I added a change of clothes or at least spare pants. I made several mini diaper kits and stashed one in the Baby Jogger, one in our child-carry backpack, and another in the glove box of the car. Then, whenever we went adventuring, I wouldn't need that gigantic diaper bag. Also, I wouldn't need to disassemble our regular diaper bag. If you take something out, you may forget to put it back in. So when we headed out for fun, I'd toss in a bottle of formula or a bag of snacks, and we were ready for an adventure on the quick, diaper and all.

Toys

For young kids, it helps to have some type of entertainment for hikes, baby jogs, or car trips. For our kids, a musical stuffed Pooh toy tied to the backpack provided hours of entertainment on our first hikes. Hint: Don't give kids your car keys, because they will lose them. Some strollers or backpacks have tiny toy bars that serve as mini entertainment centers. Other times you can improvise. Just be sure to attach toys to the backpack or running stroller with a three- to four-inch leash (a long leash has a small risk of choking kids).

Look for small lightweight toys your kids don't play with at home; that way the toys are new and exciting. For infants, make sure it's something that they can put in their mouths. A stuffed animal or a rattle that makes noise works well. For toddlers, the staples include crayons and color books, picture books, small inexpensive dolls, or magnetic drawing boards. Avoid puzzles, because pieces will get lost. Avoid bringing irreplaceable toys or trinkets. For longer trips with toddlers, bring an art kit—a plastic box with crayons, markers, colored pencils, kid's glue, yarn bits, stencils, and other craft items. Music CDs of kids' songs or movie soundtracks work great for all ages (consider headphones). We actually have a big plastic box, our car toy box, that includes a box of crayons, color books, a few favorite paperbacks, magnetic drawing boards, and two dolls.

EATING

For infants and toddlers, bring food that your kids like at home. Don't try to get fancy, and don't stress about trying new food. Prepackaged food or that which takes no preparation works best. You may have too much to organize

Never forget snacks.

to try to prepare a large, complex meal. Keep food nutritious and healthy, but don't stress if your kid goes a day without broccoli. When my kids were little, I brought easy-to-pack, easy-to-eat food: boxed raisins, Goldfish crackers, fruit leather, apple slices, peanut butter crackers, peanut butter sandwiches, cheese sandwiches, granola bars, graham crackers, and string cheese.

For infants, you will need a bottle and formula. Bring several clean bottles if you are on a multiday trip. For toddlers, spill-proof water bottles and cups will keep their clothes, your clothes, the backpack, and the car clean and dry. Straws and small eating utensils are nice to have for restaurants. If you have a breast-feeding child, make sure to bring lots of water for mom.

Don't forget to wash your child's hands. This single task, although sometimes difficult and inconvenient, is one of the most important things you can do to keep your child healthy. If a sink and soap are not readily available, use a wet wipe or alcohol-based waterless cleanser. Keep some in the car and in the backpack.

SLEEPING

For multiday trips away from home, sleeping can be very difficult for infants and toddlers. Or it can be a breeze. Fortunately, with a little TLC, young kids can sleep almost anywhere. Most important, don't let them miss a nap or be late for bedtime. You can avoid lots of sleep problems if you stick to your routine. This means that if you're out for a day trip with your young child, you have to plan around a nap (or two if your infant still takes two daily naps). For toddlers, this usually means you have to plan an outdoor activity in the morning so you are back to the car or at home for nap or quiet time. Most parents know it helps to bring a sleep buddy, usually a favorite stuffed animal or doll from home.

For overnight trips, we bring my kids' favorite pillowcases from home also. You can stuff them with clothes or put a hotel pillow inside. This way, it gives kids more of a feel of their own beds. Also, try to keep bedtime and the evening routine similar to that of home. Read books, take a bath, or play a quiet game. Remember, on most overnight adventures, especially when camping, you won't have a TV and VCR handy.

SPECIAL EQUIPMENT: STROLLERS, BACKPACKS, FRONTPACKS

For adventures with toddlers and infants, special equipment for outdoor parents can make your trips fun for both kids and adults. In fact, some things are almost mandatory. These items work so well, you might find yourself using them on a daily basis right at home.

A child-carry back-pack is a good way to take a young one hiking.

Child-Carry Backpack

The child-carry backpack is ubiquitous among outdoor and urban adventurers. It's one modern parenting device I found indispensable when my kids were little. As a parent, you will love the option of putting your child on your back and having your hands free. This allows you to go on hikes or travel through airports without worrying about carrying your child or holding his or her hand. My kids and I liked the backpack so much we never used an umbrella stroller, even when we went to the grocery store. The backpack stayed in our family car for the better part of three years.

A variety of child-carry backpacks are on the market. The inexpensive backpacks usually fit well and work great for most day trips. Make sure the pack has a harness system for kids to keep them snug, especially if you trip on a curb. Also, it's nice to have padded and adjustable straps and a waist belt for mom or dad.

The higher-end backpacks have features that my wife and I thought were indispensable. We loved having an extra pocket for diapers, wet wipes, snacks, and water. The Kelty Explorer we used had a zip-off diaper-bag backpack that we could carry separately. Ours also came with a sun shade and rain shield that I felt was important to keep kids cool and out of the sun or dry in sprinkles. It's nice if the kid's seat is adjustable so that as your child grows, he or she can still sit in the backpack comfortably. Ours also came with a complete mosquito net.

Check the various brands to compare prices and accessories. You might also be able to find a used one from friends or family.

Running Stroller

Running strollers or Baby Joggers are another great way to get out with your kids. Unlike regular strollers, running strollers have wide, beefy wheels that are inflatable, similar to those used on mountain bikes. They have sturdy aluminum frames and thick, durable canvas seats. These features allow parents to go running and jogging with their kids. We used our running stroller once or twice a week for almost two years with our first

Double Baby Jogger provides respite for kids and a workout for mom and dad.

child. I loved it so much that when we had our second child, I got a double running stroller. My kids sit side by side, and I sweat more than ever since I push nearly eighty pounds. It's a great workout. Some companies even make a triple running stroller. When my kids were little, they went on many forest trails, dirt roads, bike paths, and beach and neighborhood runs with me. Because they started in the jogger when they were young, they love it. Sometimes we even jog one mile from our house down to the ice cream store or to the library.

Running strollers come in several models, usually gauged by wheel size. Larger twenty-inch wheels allow parents to run faster over variable ground. Smaller twelve-inch wheels are more compact and easier to get in and out of your car. We used the one right in the middle with sixteen-inch wheels. That seemed to be a great compromise for running and jogging on asphalt bike paths, dirt roads, and beaches, but it is also easy enough to put in the car. It had a quick release that allowed it to fold up for storage in the car.

Most running strollers come with a sun shade and rain and wind guard. The rain/wind shield totally encases the kids in a weatherproof cocoon. Even if it is blustery or raining, your kids will be warm and dry. My kids loved cruising through the rain. Most strollers have pockets for food, snacks, water, milk, and toys. A three- or five-point harness keeps kids snug and safe.

There are a several brands: Baby Jogger is the one I liked best. Also, there is a used market for these, so look on the internet or ask your friends for a used one. You can sell yours when your kids outgrow it.

Child-Carry Frontpack

You have one more option for toting your young infant: a frontpack. Unlike backpacks, frontpacks don't get your child totally out of the way. They hold your child against your abdomen using straps that cross your back. Kids face forward in a harness that keeps them snug on your stomach. For younger, lighter kids, the frontpack sometimes is a more secure option than a backpack. They will outgrow the frontpack at around twenty pounds. This is an option for short ventures, but it is often too difficult to go far with a child strapped this way.

I don't recommend front slings for adventuring. These cloth straps keep your infant in front and against your abdomen and chest. But they don't have any straps or devices to keep your child restrained without your hands supporting him or her. You have to hold your infant with at least one hand at all times. This works okay for casual activities but not if you need your hands free.

Squishy and smelly, the aquarium touch pool is fun for a rainy day.

ON THE ROAD

Most parents will keep the first outdoor adventures close to home. Thus you will be going by car. It's nice having a car for a home base that includes lots of food, water, clothes, toys, games, and any special sports equipment like bikes or a Baby Jogger. If you go by air, you might be limited to the bare minimum. Here are some helpful hints that pertain mostly to infants and toddlers.

By Car

Keep your first trips close to home. Those that are thirty minutes away or less are generally easier. Almost any child can be entertained for half an hour in the car. For longer trips, plan at least part of the drive during nap or quiet time. This might be in the morning or perhaps in the afternoon. It helps to schedule only one activity per day, either morning or afternoon.

During the drive, keep the toys, activities, water bottles, and snacks within reach of your kids. It's very dangerous to service your children while you're behind the wheel. I have two kids with their car seats placed on the outboard positions in the backseat. In the middle, I have an inexpensive plastic dishpan that serves as the car toy box. Each of my kids' car seats has cup holders. Before the drive, I make sure their water bottles, toys, and snacks are within reach. If your car doesn't have a reading light, then consider buying a small flashlight for your child if you do some driving at night. Don't forget, if your child is potty trained, visit the toilet before getting in the car.

For longer trips, plan to have lunch in the car or stop at a park along the way to break up the drive. We plan a stop at a park or at the zoo when we make the three-hour drive to the coast. This lets the kids run around and keeps them from getting cranky. After the stop, we feed them lunch in the car while driving. This keeps them busy for another half hour. Then a quick nap, a short activity from the car toy box, and we're pulling into the campground before they know it.

By Plane

Air travel can also be quite complicated or refreshingly simple. First, when planning a trip with little kids, keep naptime and mealtimes in mind when you make your reservations. You don't want to be transferring between planes at lunchtime without enough time to eat. Try to find a nonstop flight and one that doesn't leave too early or get in too late. Travel at off-peak times during the year to avoid business travelers, and avoid holidays too. If you can afford the extra price, it may be well worth paying a bit more money or spending a bit more time to arrange your air itinerary to be as easy as possible.

Always try to be thrifty with packing. Use a backpack carry-on so your hands are free to attend to your child. Keep toys, diapers, snacks, and water handy at all times. Milk is usually available on the plane, but it helps to bring a straw or an empty spill-proof cup or bottle. Bring small portable toys that your kids will enjoy. For a special treat, try to get toys or activities from the flight attendant as well. Such toys or activities might include stickers, postcards, playing cards, or color books. It helps to feed your children before the flight and let them run around and get some exercise before flights or during layovers.

If your kids are small, they might not need a ticket. The so-called lap infant can be very difficult for the parent and the child. You will save money by having a lap infant, and it might be okay for a one- or two-hour flight. But it can be very difficult, especially for longer flights. If you travel during off-peak times, though, you may be able to use an extra seat.

Don't forget, bring your car seat on the plane. First of all, air travel is safer with a car seat, even if there is mild turbulence. Second, your child will be at home in the car seat. They will like the familiar feel of their own car seat. Any car seat that is approved for an automobile will be accepted by

Don't Forget!

- Bring your kids' favorite blanket, pillowcase, or stuffed animal when away from home.
- Bring one or two toys that are inexpensive (they will get lost, guaranteed).
- Remember to put on sunscreen and cover up before you head into the sun.
- Don't forget a change of clothes, water, snacks, and milk or formula.
- Bring lots of resealable freezer bags for food, dirty diapers, and toys.
- Take lots of wet wipes and waterless hand cleaner.
- Wash hands before meals and after bathroom stops.
- For car trips with toddlers still potty training, consider bringing a portable potty for the car. You can have a quick pit stop anywhere.
- Bring your car seat for air trips.

any airline. We took our kids to Mexico when they were one and three years old. We strapped their car seats in the plane, and they were happy as clams. On the way home our flight was delayed. We left Mexico late, and the kids fell asleep in their car seats in the Los Angeles airport. We carried them to the plane in their car seats, and they slept on the flight home. In fact, when we arrived at our home airport, we transferred them into the luggage cart and then into our car, and all the while they slept in their car seats.

Lodging and Rental Car

For trips by air in which you will be staying in a hotel and renting a car, arrange as much as possible beforehand. When you book your rental car, don't skimp on a tiny budget model, unless you don't plan on using the car much. Get a car that is big enough for luggage, backpacks, and car seats. If your car becomes your home away from home, you might find yourself changing lots of diapers in the back and even serving lunch there too. If you are going directly to the hotel and will be staying there for a week, book a shuttle to be waiting for you when your plane arrives, and forget about the hassle of a car. Don't forget to book your return shuttle to the airport when you arrive at a hotel.

Arrange your hotel well in advance. Try to find a kid-friendly hotel. An indoor pool is nice for foul weather days or spare time. It is a bonus, or sometimes a necessity, to have a hotel within walking distance of restaurants or activities. For example, if you can walk to the beach or the ski slopes, it sometimes can make the difference between an easy hassle-free day and a major headache every time you want to go somewhere.

Check on day-care options before you go if you need some adult time. Beach or winter resorts often have quality day cares.

Adventure Abroad: Special Issues for International Travel

When we took our first trip to Baja, Mexico, our kids were quite young. We took a flight that left early in the morning and had a layover around lunchtime at the Los Angeles airport. Then we arrived in La Paz around 2 P.M. with our kids rested from napping on the flight. We picked up our luggage and our driver was waiting for us at the airport. He helped us lug bags, car seats, and windsurfing gear to the huge van. As we had previously arranged, the driver stopped at the supermercado in La Paz so we could buy six bags of groceries. While my wife shopped, the kids and I had a snack at a nearby park. Then, we settled in the van for a forty-five-minute drive to the remote village of La Ventana. I sat in the back so I could interact with our children, pointing out houses, fields of peppers, and the occasional stray dog. Our casita, a small beach cabin, was ready when we arrived at 4 P.M., and we unpacked the groceries and stepped outside our front door onto the beach. It was so smooth we weren't sure what happened.

International trips can be exciting and loads of fun for the whole family. At the same time, overseas travel with kids takes a bit more time and preparation. Fortunately, with the internet and phones, you can book your entire trip before you go, including lodging, campgrounds, rental cars, excursions, and equipment rental. Not only can you investigate family-friendly facilities, but you can also find out if other families liked or disliked certain activities, restaurants, or hotels. It's really important to book as much as possible ahead of time. As with any adventure, timing is important too. You don't want to fly into a foreign country at midnight and then try to find a hotel. Also, look into packages that include air, lodging, ground transportation, meals, and equipment rentals like bikes, canoes, or camping gear. This makes life a lot easier, and it may be less expensive. Some travel agencies have discounts for families or let kids stay for no extra charge.

Experiencing new culture includes airplane food.

GO LIGHT AND PRACTICE

International travel requires much preparation, as does any trip. I won't repeat the planning and packing tips I already discussed in previous chapters, but in today's world, safety and health are paramount. You want to have a memorable trip, and everyone should have fun, parents too. To do that when traveling to a foreign country, you have to take some time with planning and packing. Since my family takes one international trip every year or two, I tend to start the planning process a year in advance. When my friends came back from a Mexico trip to a family-friendly surf town, I got detailed information about what worked and what didn't. Then I went home and searched the internet for more info. I took notes, with special attention to the beach cabin, family restaurants that were within walking distance of the cabin, and the location of the supermarket. The notes went into my file for future reference.

Try to find kid-friendly hotels, family hostels, or resorts used to groups. It is best to have a nice place to stay if the weather is bad or you need a down day. With young kids, it is often better to be centrally located so you don't have to drive much or ride a bus to get to the beach or park. Even if you have to pay a bit more, it is often easier to walk a few blocks than to ride a bus ten minutes. For beach or winter resorts, I search for hotels in which we can easily walk to the grocery store, family restaurants, and the beach or snow. Alternatively, get a rental car instead of trying to take the bus or a taxi everywhere. Also, it's nice to have a hotel with a kitchenette.

I recommend a small stash of emergency food. You don't have to bring a suitcase full, but throw in a few granola bars, fruit leather, crackers, or whatever snacks your child likes that might not be available where you are going. For example, we bring powdered Ovaltine for chocolate milk. This provides a smile, curbs hunger, and gives kids extra vitamins wherever we can find milk.

Bring your own car seat. You won't likely find one where you are going. Sometimes rental car companies can provide them, but don't count on it. It is a hassle to bring a car seat, but the risk is too great not to have one. We went to Baja with two seats in tow. We used them on the plane, and my kids had a better airplane ride because they were in their familiar car seats— "Just like at home!" Then we used both seats in the van shuttle to the beach cabin we rented. Once there, we strapped the seats to the dining chairs in the community kitchen: They made perfect booster seats for eating.

Be advised, diapers and pull-ups may not be available in certain areas or in the developing world. Bring wet wipes too. They are handy to keep your kids' bottoms clean, but they also work great to wash their hands before meals when there is no bathroom or running water handy. You can also give kids a "sponge bath" with wet wipes: clean their faces, hands, feet, and bottoms before bed. Also, bring travel-size containers of baby shampoo, body wash, waterless gel cleaner, and lotion.

It may be difficult to sterilize bottles and spill-proof cups overseas. Whenever possible, wash them in hot soapy water and rinse them thoroughly. To sterilize, you probably need to boil them. Consider soaking overnight in water treated with a water purification tablet or a few drops of chlorine bleach if you are in the developing world. It's better to wean your kids off bottles and sippy cups as soon as you can.

Bring a backpack. Your over-the-shoulder diaper bag may work at home, but you will want both hands free when traveling abroad. In busy markets or airports, you'll want one hand holding your child's at all times. It's best to keep enough room in the diaper bag for the day's snacks, water, and camera. That way you don't have to bring a separate lunch bag or camera kit.

I found the diaper-bag backpack that zipped on the child-carry backpack indispensable when I traveled abroad with my young kids. My youngest child and the diaper bag were on my back. With one hand I held my toddler, and the other a rolling duffel bag. I never let go of my kids through airports or markets.

Dress children alike. I hated wearing the same clothes as my brother and sister on a trip to Disneyland when I was seven years old. But if it helps you keep track of your kids, it is worth a few complaints. Remember, in today's world you can't be too safe. Make a game out of it or give your kids a reward if they don't complain about dressing alike. You can pick different clothing, but use the same color. Alternatively, pick the same pattern or style of top, with different colors. It is amazing how handy this will be when keeping track of your kids in busy airports, amusement parks, or open markets. If you are really bold, dress yourself like your kids.

Pack light. Nothing's worse than hauling pounds of gear to the airport, rental car counter, and hotel (and then trying to get it all home again). Limit luggage to whatever you can carry while holding children's hands. My wife and I each carry one rolling duffel bag and wear one backpack. That way, we each hold one of our kids' hands. You'll be surprised how much you can live without for a week of traveling.

On one overseas trip to the tropics with my young kids, my whole family packed one large duffel bag with wheels. On arrival, we inquired about the local laundry facilities. For five dollars per load, we had washed, dried, and folded clothes every third day. You can always wash underwear and socks in the hotel sink too. Bring some no-rinse soap for doing a few key items, such as underpants, in the hotel sink. Also, you can buy a souvenir T-shirt or two if you run out of clothes.

Packing Light Is Right

Here are some tips for lightweight luggage.
- Mom or dad's coat can do double duty as a blanket.
- Long underwear or sweats will work as pajamas.
- Polypropylene tops can be worn in water for sun protection and as sweatshirts for cool evenings. They dry quickly, are easy to wash, and are quite warm.
- Do laundry every third or fourth day, or wash underwear and socks in the hotel sink.

Practice traveling. It might sound silly, but if you are heading abroad, you and your kids should have some experience at traveling. Practice eating out and spending the night away from home. Practice with airports, rental cars, and hotels on domestic trips. In other words, don't make your first big trip with the kids a two-week ski trip to Europe or a beach trip to Mexico. Do local trips when kids are young; let the kids and yourself get accustomed to travel. The more trips you do, the easier they will become. Save overseas adventures for after you become adventure pros.

BEFORE YOU GO

I've talked about planning and packing for adventures and given special tips. However, international travel requires extra steps. Here are a few vital items regarding travel abroad. You don't want to forget these special issues.

Passport

Your kids should have their own passports. If mom and dad split up for any reason, possibly for an emergency, your child should have his or her own passport so he or she can go with either parent.

Notarized Letter from Nontraveling Spouse

If you are a single parent traveling with a child, many countries require a notarized letter signed by the other parent. The parent staying home needs to give you permission to travel with your child solo. This is a requirement in Mexico and other countries. Unfortunately, many people learn the hard way. The airline might not let you on the flight exiting the U.S., and you could be stuck in an airport waiting for the letter. My friend drove to Baja, while his wife and kids flew down a week later. His wife and children got stuck in Los Angeles while they tried to track him down in Cabo San Lucas to get the letter. Fortunately, it only delayed their trip for a couple days.

Other Forms

Check the country you are visiting to see what requirements are necessary. You may need a tourist card or visa. Get these well in advance. Some countries do not issue these promptly. It may take several weeks.

Extra Passport Photos and Passport Photocopy

If you lose your passport, having a photocopy of the photo page plus a spare photo for you and your kids can make getting a replacement much easier. Store it in a separate bag away from your passport.

Money

Everyone has a different philosophy when it comes to carrying money overseas. For international trips, I always have enough cash to handle a minor emergency. I bring a credit card for most major purchases and have an extra credit card hidden in my luggage for a backup. Finally, I always bring traveler's checks. They are almost as good as cash, and they can be replaced if lost or stolen.

Itinerary

Leave your itinerary with friends or family members, especially contact numbers where they can reach you in an emergency. It's nice to check in once you get there. Find an internet café or make a quick phone call.

Immunizations and Immunization Record

You may need to get special shots or take special medicine before visiting certain countries, such as those in Africa. In much of the tropics, you may need to take medicine to prevent malaria. You may have to show proof of immunization to enter the country or to return home.

The immunizations your child needs depend on where you are traveling to, the age of your child, how long you are staying, your child's previous immunizations, and other factors. It's best to check with your doctor or a travel health clinic.

Medical and Diplomatic Facilities

Get the name, phone number, and address of hospitals and the U.S. embassy or consulate in whatever country and town you are visiting. This will take just a few minutes on the internet. You will probably never need it, but if anything comes up, it will save you lots of time and frustration.

Tourist Bureau

The local tourist bureau can be helpful if you have travel or lodging problems. They can also assist with planning activities or excursions.

Medical Kit Additions

Depending on where you are going, you may need to add certain medicines to your first aid kit. If you travel to Nepal or Chile, for example, you might bring some medicine for acute mountain sickness. If you travel to the tropics, malaria prophylaxis and traveler's diarrhea medicine may be necessary. Check with your doctor before you go. Make sure all prescription medicines are in their appropriate bottles, with your or your child's name on them.

This applies to regular prescription medicines for chronic illnesses like asthma as well as a "just in case" antibiotic prescription that your doctor may provide you with.

TRAVEL HEALTHY

One final bit of information will make your international adventure more likely to succeed. Stay healthy. Having a sick child or parent in a foreign country is no fun. No one wants to hole up in a hotel room while everyone else is sightseeing or playing on the beach. Two big risks for illness when abroad are food and hygiene. Here are some tips that apply to any adventure, domestic or international. They are vitally important when traveling overseas to the developing world.

- Food should always be washed, peeled, cooked, and served hot. For kids, stick to familiar foods like grilled cheese or pasta. Avoid meat if there is any question about its source or if it is not fully cooked. For example, burgers should be completely cooked until they are brown (well done) and they should be served hot.
- Bring your own utensils and clean them after meals. A small fork and spoon from home may help your child eat too.
- Water must be pure (see chapter 2 on purification). Bottled water, juice, and soft drinks are probably okay. If you order bottled water, make sure the seal is not broken. Some restaurants in the developing world have been known to refill water bottles with tap water that could be contaminated.
- Milk should be pasteurized. If you're not sure, don't drink it. You can bring powdered milk from home. Alternatively, find canned milk.
- Proper hygiene is very important, especially in the bathroom. Kids should wash their hands after going to the bathroom and before meals. Use wet wipes or alcohol-based waterless gel to clean their bottoms and hands.
- Always wear shoes to avoid cuts and scrapes.
- Protect skin from sun and insects.

Part 2

OUTDOOR ADVENTURE

I have many fond memories of the outdoors as a child. Even at a young age, I spent time with my dad hunting and fishing in our favorite Pacific Northwest haunts. We always went on an annual family ski trip; I participated in the family trip even after I left home for college. One of my fondest memories is digging razor clams: Every spring we'd take a long weekend and go to the rugged Washington State coast. We'd wake up at dawn, stumble out to the cold Pacific shore, and dig razor clams with clam guns—long, round tubes designed for just such a purpose. The waves splashed over my boot tops and doused my feet in chilly water. We'd comb the sand and yell "I got one!" after a successful dig. I'd help my little sisters dig clams after I obtained my limit. After an hour we'd huddle inside our beach cottage or cabin, eat breakfast, and plan the rest of the day: play capture the flag in the dunes, have sand castle contests on the beach, bike around town, or shop for saltwater taffy.

Now, both my young daughters love sports and adventure. We have tried a lot of different adventures in the last few years. We swim twice a week year-round and take our bikes on every weekend outing. My kids have their favorites—my youngest, Avrie, can't wait to go skiing in the winter. She loves the wind in her face. Once, she didn't want to quit and eventually fell asleep on the chairlift, exhausted and smiling. My oldest daughter, Skylar, gets more excited about camping. She loves making a shopping list and gathering camping gear, especially the tent and her sleeping bag. Both kids are almost always excited for any new trip or outing, so long as I am.

Remember, teaching your child a new skill or sport—watching them soak it up, apply it, and move on the next challenge—is one of the deep thrills and joys of parenting. These chapters are all about that reward, being outside in the sun, wind, rain, and snow, playing with your kids, and educating them on science, history, and culture. Teach and have fun. Learn and play. Be bold yet cautious, enthusiastic, and curious. Wild kids are truly a blast. Get ready and hold on for the adventure of your life.

In part 1, I reviewed the formula for success: Plan ahead, do some basic preparation, and stay organized. Remember, simple is good and supervision is mandatory. The more you go, the easier it gets. And it really isn't that difficult.

Part 2 covers the most common outdoor adventure sports. They include activities for all seasons, all budgets, and all ages, possibly including grandma and grandpa. Some are great for one-on-one with your teen. Others work well for large blended or extended families. You might start with basics like hiking or biking. Then you might venture to camping, backpacking, or water sports. There is something here for everyone.

I've tried all these sports as a child, adult, and parent. For the most part, they are fun and safe. You'll notice that each chapter discusses necessary equipment, basic skills, and safety issues. Try something, and if it doesn't seem to be working, give yourself and your family a break. Try another activity at another time. It doesn't really matter what activity you choose, even one not specifically listed here. The main point is to have fun and make memories.

Hiking

My family loves hiking—it's simple, easy, and everyone can do it. Our favorites are short hikes that don't take much planning, packing, or preparation. We make lunch, don our hiking clothing, and grab our rain boots. Often we hike at a local nature preserve called Catherine's Creek that's a half hour's drive from our house. This wildland is packed with blooming flowers, good scrambling rocks, and a small brook. Once we went to Catherine's Creek with Skylar's school on a field trip to collect tadpoles. Another time it was pouring buckets of rain so we played in the rain for half an hour and then made a beeline for home and dry clothes. We go with grandma and grandpa once a year to view the blooming purple wisteria.

Be adventurous: Pick longer hikes, more challenging terrain, and different locales farther from home. Or be lackluster: Simple and short is okay. You'll be amazed at what wonders your kids will find or what fun they can have on a simple walk through the woods. You can hike in almost every community: Choose from nature boardwalks, walking paths, or hiking trails. Go with all ages and all skill levels; take friends or your entire large, extended or mixed families.

With smaller children, hiking can be a wonderful activity. But keep in mind you won't go as far as you do when you hike on your own. Plan to stop for every flower, pile of dirt, large rock, bird's nest, or interesting tree. I remember our first hike for the summer with both kids: Avrie was two, Skylar five. We set out with a backpack full of lunch and hiked about three hundred yards to a waterfall for a picnic. We spent an hour playing at the waterfall, eating lunch, and watching squirrels. Then we went three hundred yards back to the car and home.

If you have older kids, get in shape. They will want to cruise on the trail, and the hike could turn into a great workout.

The whole clan out for a hike, one all ages can enjoy.

GEARING UP

Day or half-day hiking trips require only a good backpack, food and water, adequate footwear, and some basic emergency supplies. Fortunately, you don't need a lot of special gear. You probably have everything already. Let's look at the basics first.

Day Pack

A day pack, also called a rucksack or backpack, should be worn by everyone, except perhaps small kids. Even school-age kids can wear a small pack and carry their lunch and a small water bottle. It's fun for them to carry some of the supplies, and it starts a good habit: Always carry some basic provisions of food, water, spare clothing, and emergency supplies. Be prepared to carry the backpack of your preschooler or kindergartner.

Most kids already have a backpack or school bag. This will work just fine for short hikes. You don't need to buy a separate hiking backpack unless you plan on hiking a lot or unless you don't have a school bag. There are a multitude of backpacks made for kids. Get one that is not too big for their bodies. Older kids might like packs with special pockets for water bottles, hydration bladders, or CD or MP3 players. But don't spend too much.

For adults, get a good quality backpack that is large enough to carry some of the family's food, water, and extra clothing. If your kids are young, they might not be able to fit more than a lunch and water in their packs. If

Hiking Safety

Hiking safety is paramount. I always have a fun chat or briefing before I head out with my kids. I inform them that there are certain rules for hiking. But I make the talk fun, and we laugh. Every time before we head out I tell them, "We need to talk," and they laugh and say, "Oh, Dad, not again." Here are our basic rules.

- Always stay together. If one person needs to stop, everyone stops.
- Take regular breaks for food, water, and rests. Sometimes I have to make my kids stop and take a break, even a brief one.
- Everyone brings extra clothing. When I say it's time to put on a sun hat or raincoat, they know that that is one of the rules. My kids are young, so sometimes they greatly resist a hat or coat, even in a downpour. Let's face it, it's fun to get wet, as long as you are not an hour's hike from the car.
- Know the trail. I always bring a map and compass. Older kids will love it if you go over the trail map before and during the hike. You can even make notations on the map, such as the location of a neat waterfall or the spot where you saw a deer. Remember, if you don't know how to use a map and compass, they are useless. My youngest loves looking at maps, even though she doesn't know exactly how to read them. Someday, though, she'll be an expert at orienteering.
- Bring a basic first aid and survival kit (see chapters 17 and 18). "Do we have it?" I ask. "Check!" yell my daughters. They also carry a flashlight and whistle.
- Bring a cell phone or Family Radio Station (FRS, a portable walkie-talkie) radio, which is handy for emergencies. Remember, there is nothing wrong with teaching your child how to dial 911 on the cell phone so long as they know it's only to be used in an emergency. For FRS radios, some public agencies monitor channel 9, security code 11.

they want to take off their coats, you should be able to stuff them in your pack. For most adults, a pack that is 1,500 or 2,000 cubic inches will work fine. If you have a large family or you hike a lot in marginal weather, when you need lots of extra clothes (which tend to be bulky), consider a 2,000- to 3,000-cubic-inch pack. You can find these at outdoor and retail stores.

Big packs up a tough trail:
Hiking is an all-time
family favorite.

Water

Water is very important. I think it's a good idea for kids to get used to carrying their own. The easiest way is to have your children carry a small water bottle designed for biking or hiking. These are usually spill-proof and easy to drink from. Smaller kids may need bottles with small spouts.

Older kids may prefer hydration bladders. These are vinyl or plastic water bladders. A long hose or tube runs from the bladder, which is stashed in the pack, to the shoulder strap. If you or your child needs a drink, simply suck on the tube; a one-way valve keeps it from dripping.

Remember, if you get water from a stream, it should be treated as mentioned in chapter 2. It's best to bring enough water for your whole trip.

Food

What and how much food you bring largely depends on personal tastes and the length of your trip. Some families prefer to take a regular lunch. Sandwiches are the easiest to pack and eat, plus they are the most durable: Most kids think they still taste just fine, even if the sandwich is a bit squashed from lying in the bottom of the backpack. Young kids might wrinkle their noses at a sandwich that has been flattened too much, so pack carefully. Pack lunch in a reusable plastic food storage container.

Some families, especially those with older kids on longer hikes, tend to snack all day without taking a specific lunch break. This sometimes works better. First, you don't need to take the time to sit and eat. Sometimes this delays your hike or kids get cold. Second, you don't have to spend the time to digest a large meal, and you avoid that tired feeling after a big meal.

I remember days hunting with my father, when we'd have a huge breakfast before dawn and then eat randomly throughout the day while hiking up hillsides, streambeds, and canyons. We never got hungry or tired. We would snack on granola bars, fruit, and our staple, crackers sandwiched with peanut butter.

Whether you stop for lunch or snack, bring a bit more food than you think you need. This will come in handy for an unexpected delay, for an extra-hungry child, or the kid who left lunch sitting on the hood of the car. There's nothing worse than hiking the last hour back to the car with a hungry child or parent. Toss in backup food like a prepackaged granola bar, dried fruit, or turkey jerky.

Shoes

For hiking, everyone should have good quality footwear. Depending on how far you hike and what the conditions are, you have a wide choice of shoes. For short hikes, one or two hours on an easy flat trail, tennis shoes may suffice. You already have them for your kids, so you won't need to buy special shoes. Plus they are lightweight and inexpensive. However, for longer hikes in which you may encounter mud, rocks, stream crossings, or other obstacles, hiking boots are better. Short-top canvas hiking shoes are light and comfortable. Mid- or high-top boots provide more support and protection from the elements.

Remember, good boots need to be worn a few times to soften the flex. Otherwise you or your kids could get blisters. With new boots or old ones, you still should watch for blisters on the trail. Stop early if there is a sore spot, before it's a blister. Stick a piece of tape or moleskin on the hot spot. Adjust the boot's fit or put on a clean, dry pair of socks.

Clothing

As mentioned in chapter 2, you need warm clothes and rain gear or a parka for foul weather. The basic rule is to take at least one extra piece of clothing beyond what you and your kids are wearing when you leave the car. Usually this means you will toss in a coat or rain jacket. If you're already wearing a jacket, pack an extra fleece sweatshirt. If you are hiking in wet conditions, it is a good idea to throw in an extra pair of socks. If the temperature is cool, bring a hat and gloves for everyone.

PLANNING A ROUTE

Planning a route to hike should be pretty simple. Look for hiking trails in your community by checking local guidebooks, maps, ranger stations, tourist offices, or the internet. Also, ask your friends. We've hit good trail hikes solely on suggestions from friends. It's nice if other families tested a trail first, but it's even better if they take you along and show it to you and your family.

If you are visiting a state or national park, national forest, or other public recreation area, check in at the ranger station. It's important to study maps and guidebooks, but also talk to the rangers. Tell them exactly what you are looking for, especially the ages of your kids. Oftentimes they can provide an excellent trail recommendation. Plus, they know the local and seasonal conditions. Mudslides or downed timber might not be listed in a trail map or guidebook, but such obstacles can render a trail useless.

Here are a few tips for planning a hike to help make your first trip enjoyable.

Start with an easy trail in a well-known area for your first outing. Don't make it too complicated. Pick a local walking path, a nature trail, or a short easy hiking trail.

When starting out, choose a hike that goes out and back. In other words, it goes to a specific destination, then you turn around and hike the same trail back to your car. This allows you to turn around at any point and head home if you have any problems like a tired child, foul weather, or a trail washout. Loop hikes are fun because you don't see the same scenery twice, but you can't just zip back home if you are more than halfway through the loop and the trail is blocked from downed timber or mudslides. Backtracking can take much longer than you planned.

Always have a backup plan for foul weather. In other words, if you drive an hour just to find buckets of rain falling, head to an indoor play area or museum instead. It is okay to let your kids experience disappointment, but don't ruin the whole day just because the weather turns icky. Choose an alternative and let your kids know the trail will be around for another day.

Timing is very important when hiking, especially with younger kids. Our best hikes start like this: We pack our gear the night before, have a good breakfast and pack lunch that morning at home, and drive to the trailhead early in the day. That way we can hike in the morning, eat lunch on

Kids are fascinated with anything, even a trail culvert.

the trail, and head back in early afternoon. We do most of our hiking in the morning when everyone is fresh. We're often back to the car just after lunch, so my kids still get quiet time during the afternoon drive home. This also gives us a time buffer. We have plenty of time to get back before dark and have several hours of daylight if we have any problems.

Don't fill up the whole day. For a day hike, we usually aim for no more than two hours of hiking with younger kids. With older kids, you can go up to six hours. It's nice to have a buffer of time: Perhaps in nice weather you will take a side trail to a waterfall or take an extra long lunch to sit in the sun and chat with your kids. If the weather looks lousy, it's nice to have an option to cut your hike short. Even with eager teens, don't plan to be hiking from dawn to dusk. You may be hiking out at dark if you get delayed for any reason. The most common delay is not a mishap but when hikers are having so much fun they lose track of time.

When planning a hike, remember that your speed and distance will be variable. You may hike anywhere from a half mile to three or four miles an hour, depending on the age and physical conditioning of the kids. Also, taking stops to investigate bird nests, waterfalls, or animal droppings can add time. You shouldn't miss these opportunities because you are pressed for time. Young kids as a rule like to lollygag. Older kids often like to press onward.

ON THE TRAIL

Hiking is pretty simple. Anyone can do it, from young kids to grandparents. It's a great activity, especially for extended, blended, or large families. Here are some time-tested trail tips.

Hiking pace is important. Generally you hike only as fast as the slowest person. In other words, keep a good rhythm, but make sure everyone sticks together. It's good to keep moving, but don't be so strict that you can't stop to check out blooming flowers or a cool rock formation. That's why I like an out-and-back hike. Sometimes everyone will be in a mood to just hike, and you'll have completed a four-mile hike before you know it. Other times, your family will stroll along the trail, and you'll spend more time eating lunch in the sun than hiking. Just go with the flow, and see how everyone feels that day. Maybe this will be a good time to talk with your teen about school or friends. Maybe everyone will need to blow off steam and hike in the peace and quiet of the forest.

Remember to take plenty of breaks for food, water, and rest. In general, it's best to stop every thirty minutes or so with younger kids. Older kids can go an hour before they need a break. It's okay to keep breaks short, to five or ten minutes. You don't have to snack all day long, but kids do need to

Make sure you allot time for plenty of breaks.

Special Activities

There are some additional activities you can do on the trail to make things fun. You don't necessarily need an activity other than hiking, but sometimes it is fun to have a focus for the hike. It can keep young kids interested, and it gives teens a project. It can be especially helpful if you have a family member who is reluctant to participate.

- Take pictures. Digital cameras can be a blast for preschoolers and teens. Plus, when you get home, your teen can check them out on the computer and email them to friends or grandparents.
- Identify flowers or trees. Get a field guide for the local flora and fauna. Older kids will pick up this activity quickly. Younger kids may just look for certain colors or pick out one or two special flowers.
- Search for a good lunch spot with a view, a small gurgling stream, or sun spot. If the sun is hot, pick a shaded area.
- Count animals or insects, such as chipmunks, squirrels, or butterflies.
- Count rings on tree stumps. One ring is made for each year the tree was alive.
- Sing softly along the trail. Don't startle animals, but have fun with a familiar tune.

drink. You might have to remind them to get out their water bottles and take a sip with every rest.

Obstacles and hazards can be present on the trail. Watch for fallen logs, mud, deep puddles, washed out sections of trail, rocks, scree or talus slopes, swift water, waterfalls, and deep pools.

Be prepared to carry little kids. They might get tired, fussy, hungry, thirsty, or just need a bit of attention. Watch for early signs of fatigue, hunger, or thirst. Stop for a break or head back before any of your kids has a meltdown.

6

Car Camping

Every spring my family plans a beach camping trip to the Oregon coast. We also try to do a long trip to a different national park every year. In addition, we return several times a summer to our favorite standby, Lower Falls Camp. We like Lower Falls for several reasons. First, it's only an hour away from our house in a beautiful secluded section of the Gifford Pinchot National Forest. Second, my kids know the place well: They recognize the campsites, know the bike trails, and feel comfortable in the area. Third, because it's close, we can be packed and rolling within a few hours of deciding to leave. We almost always go with at least one other family, often two or three other families.

Lower Falls has everything we like about a family-friendly campground. It has huge old-growth shade trees and several bike trails. It has river access that is protected by railings and stairs. The campground roads are wide, circular, and smooth: perfect for biking, with good visibility for cars that are driving through. The campsites are all kid-friendly: large sites with minimal rocks and stumps. Also, the fire pits are protected with cast iron grills and are set away from the tent areas and the trees.

So what is car camping, exactly? In car camping, you set up your tent right next to your car; thus you have the luxury of bringing a carload of gear, unlike backpacking, in which you're limited to what you can carry on your back. With car camping, you can bring a cooler full of food, lots of extra clothes, and toys for kids and grown-ups like bikes, surfboards, a canoe, fishing poles, or whatever you choose. Car camping is a staple outdoor activity and the easiest way to head out on an overnight trip. It's also a great way to get your kids used to camping, preparing them for more advanced trips like backpacking or overseas travel.

Spring camping: Always prepare for rain.

One word of advice: I see lots of car campers who make trips too complicated by bringing too much gear, using too many complicated accessories, and spending too much time preparing food. I avoid luxury items like battery-powered or hand-crank blenders or hot water showers and coffee makers powered by your car's power point. I think these just make your trip more burdensome. Plus you'll miss out on some of the fun of getting dirty and keeping camp life simple. The idea with kids is to bring enough gear to have a fun, pleasurable trip but not be overburdened with too much gear or too many camp chores. A recurring theme in this chapter is keep it simple.

GEARING UP
No matter what size your car is, you will likely fill it to the brim. The first trip will be the most difficult, since you will bring stuff you don't need, and you will forget a few things you do need. Also, the first trip of any season tends to take extra time since you have to dig out your gear and organize it. Below is a list of the basic gear you will need, plus time-tested tips on equipment from my family and outdoor family experts.

Tent
Your tent will be your home away from home. If it is good quality and you take care of it, a tent will last years. There are many sizes, shapes, and styles. My preference is the freestanding dome tent. This style is quick to set up,

Even young kids can carry some gear on a hike.

durable, and you don't even need to stake or guy a dome tent if the weather is mild. In a rain or wind storm, they are the warmest and coziest tents around.

Because I live in the Pacific Northwest, I insist that all my tents have a full rain fly. This means the rain fly fully encapsulates the tent in a water-resistant shell. Some tents have only a partial rain fly that covers the top third of the tent, which is neither as warm nor as weatherproof as a full rain fly.

The downside of most domes is that you generally can't stand up in them because they usually are five feet high or less. Also, they are a bit more expensive. Alternatively, many campers like large, external-pole, multiroom tents: You usually can stand up in them, and they are quite roomy. Some sleep up to ten people. However, they are heavy, take up a lot of space in your car, and take some time to set up, stake, and guy with lines. Also, they are not as warm and cozy as a dome.

Rain never stopped anyone looking for chocolate milk.

Most family-size tents are four-person or larger. Keep in mind, a four-person tent has room for four people without gear or a dog. If you have a family of four, consider getting a five- or six-person tent so you have room for extra gear in the tent. This allows room for a clothing bag or a child's friend. You may want to bring two smaller tents if your kids are older: one for kids, one for mom and dad.

When my kids were young, I'd set up my fifteen-year-old beat-up mountaineering tent as the play tent. Kids love hanging out in the tent. Our play tent is always full of toys, sand, dirt, and other kids from the campground. My kids, and the rest of their campground gang, have a ball running in and out of the tent or playing house. The clean sleep tent is always off limits except for nap-, quiet-, or nighttime. We set it up and zip it closed and have a no shoes rule.

Remember when you get home to dry your tent thoroughly by hanging it in the garage. You don't want it to mildew.

Sleeping Bags

A sleeping bag is another standard piece of camping gear that, if chosen wisely, will last a long time. There are hundreds of bags on the market with various qualities, prices, and features. Depending on how old your child is, you may want to get a kid's bag, which is generally shorter and not quite as warm. Your two main choices include type of filler material (down or synthetic) and how warm a bag to buy.

Down settles closely around the skin and is warmer and cozier than synthetic sleeping-bag fill material. Down is a more efficient insulator for the same weight as synthetic and is thus lighter. It compresses into a smaller stuff sack and is more durable in the long run. Synthetic is a good choice anytime your bag might get wet or dirty. Synthetic materials are easier to clean and store. (Down should not be stored compressed in a stuff sack and should be kept clean.) Also, synthetics don't absorb as much water or sweat as down and are still quite warm even when they get damp. And finally, synthetics are cheaper initially but don't last as long. My summer down sleeping bag, for example, is in its twentieth year of use.

It's all fun lolly-gagging before bed.

Down or Synthetic Sleeping Bag?

Down is:
- Warmer by weight
- More compressible
- Lighter
- Feels better (settles next to the skin and is very soft)
- Longer lasting

Synthetic is:
- Easy to clean and store
- Warm, even when wet
- Quicker drying
- Less expensive initially
- Less absorbent

I'd recommend a synthetic-fill bag for younger kids, mainly because these bags are easier to clean and store, and they are less expensive. For older kids, if you plan on doing a lot of camping in cold weather or backpacking, you might want a down bag. A lightweight down bag also comes in handy for international travel if you need to save weight and space.

Temperature rating varies among manufacturers, quality, and style of sleeping bag, among other factors. For three-season below-timberline use, most families will choose a bag rated at 15 or 30 degrees F. If a bag is rated at 30 degrees, it means an average adult will be comfortable as long as the temperature is 30 degrees or warmer. In other words, as long as the nighttime temperature doesn't drop below freezing, you should be plenty warm. You might want a warmer bag if you tend to get cold at night or if you want to take fewer clothes. Alternatively, look for a lighter-weight 45-degree bag if you're strictly a fair-weather summer camper in warm climates. For four-season above-treeline use, most bags are rated 0 degrees and below. Mountain expedition bags are usually rated at minus 20 degrees or below.

Kids love their own bags, and you'll get plenty of use out of them for camping, traveling, and sleepovers at grandma and grandpa's house. However, if your kids are school age or preteens, you might not want to purchase a four- or five-foot-long kid's sleeping bag only to watch them grow out of it in a year or two. You can use an adult bag for kids. Just fold the lower half of the bag under them. This shortens the sleeping bag and gives them extra padding. That way, you don't have to buy them an adult bag when they get older. Keep in mind, if cared for properly, a good sleeping bag will last your kid's entire childhood.

Sleeping Pads
In addition to a quality bag, a sleeping pad is important for warmth. Snow campers know that you need a thick pad to stay warm and to get a good

night's sleep. But this applies to all outdoor families as well, even on a summer beach camping trip. Pads come in multiple thicknesses and materials.

Closed-cell foam pads are the least expensive and the most durable. These inexpensive foam pads can take a beating and still function just fine. They are light and come in many sizes. The dual-density Rainier Pad from High Country is perhaps the thickest and warmest. The two-plus inches of foam will work on cold nights, and your kids can jump on it when tentbound in a state park on a rainy day. It even comes in a two-person size.

Many backpackers prefer inflatable pads because they can be more comfortable and they pack into a smaller bundle (even though they are slightly heavier). For car camping with kids, though, they are not a necessity. Be careful with inflatables: A small puncture can leave them pancakeflat by morning. (Hint: Carry a repair kit.) The inflatable originators Cascade Designs builds an impressive array of Thermarest pads in a variety of prices, shapes, and thicknesses. You can also get a beefy inflatable mattress, which can be up to four inches thick. These can be super comfy, but you must remember to bring an electric or foot pump to inflate them.

When my kids were little, my family usually brought two adult-size pads: a two-person and a one-person pad. When lined up in the tent, the pads covered the entire floor and everyone had a spot. Now that my kids are older, everyone has their own pad.

Tips to Stay Warmer at Night

If your camping trip turns out to be a bit colder than you expected, there are several methods to keep your children warm at night. This is especially useful if you are camping in the spring and fall or anytime you feel their sleeping bags may not be warm enough. Try these options:

- Use a sleeping bag liner of silk or fleece or throw a blanket over the top of your kid's sleeping bag.
- Have your kids wear synthetic long underwear and socks or thick pajamas with feet.
- Put a hat on your child.
- Use a thicker pad.
- Bring a warmer tent. Generally, smaller tents with fewer mesh panels are warmer, especially if they have a rain fly.
- Eat a snack or high-calorie beverage like hot chocolate before bed. (Just make sure your kids brush their teeth.)

Cooking Gear

When you are car camping, unlike backpacking, you'll have the luxury of taking extra cooking gear and plenty of food. But you don't want to be loaded down with too many fancy items. A common mistake among novice families is that they spend more time preparing food and cooking in camp than they do at home.

We keep meals simple, nutritious, and familiar. Pancakes and oatmeal are as fancy as we get for breakfast. Lunches are usually sandwiches, chips, fruit, and veggies. Dinners are planned in advance so everything can be cooked with two pots. See the sidebar for my family's favorite menu ideas. Here's a sample of what you will need for your complete, but simple, car camp chuck box. You may make additions or deletions to this list, but here's what I take for a two-day or two-week trip.

- Camp stove: two-burner, folding propane stove
- Propane canister or refillable bottle
- Nonstick frying pan
- Cook pots, usually set of three that are nestled together and come with handles and lids
- Small kettle with handle, pour spout, and lid
- Plastic colander for draining pasta, washing veggies, or serving sliced fruit
- Plastic spatula and large serving spoon
- Lexan flatwear: forks, knives, spoons (bring extra for camp dinner guests)
- Plastic or paper plates—although it's nice to have reusable plastic plates, sometimes paper plates are better, since you don't need hot water or soap to clean them; metal plates are nifty, but they make your cook box heavy
- Plastic bowls—these are especially helpful when kids eat anything that can be messy or if they have to hold their food on their lap.
- Small cutting board and knife—the knife should be stored in a plastic knife holder so no one is inadvertently poked when reaching into the cook box
- Plastic dish tub and hand towels
- Paper towels and wet wipes
- Small container of dish soap and waterless alcohol-based hand cleaner
- Salt, pepper, and small bottle of olive or canola oil
- Plastic drinking cups and coffee cups
- Coffee maker—get something simple like a thermo-french press or a cone drip system

Our Favorite Camp Meals

We keep food simple. For breakfast we cook either oatmeal or pancakes. A nutritious hot breakfast goes a long way toward starting out the day right.

For lunch, we eat no-cook meals like sandwiches or leftovers from dinner the night before. Like at home, we have chips, veggies, olives, sliced fruit, and crackers.

For dinner, we keep things simple. Have I said that before? There's no reason to get too complex when camping. Also, I love to cook one meal that my kids and my wife and I will eat. Otherwise, you might find yourself making two complete dinners.

Spaghetti, salad, and bread are easy to prepare ahead of time and take minimal effort when camping. Heat up the sauce and cook the noodles. Depending on their mood, my kids might have noodles plain or with sauce.

Sometimes we will cook ravioli with sauce and steamed broccoli. Cut and wash the broccoli at home and place it in a freezer bag. Prepare or buy pasta sauce before you go as well. Wrap a loaf of french bread in foil before your trip. Warm it on the campfire grill a few minutes before the rest of dinner is ready.

Another favorite dinner is chicken and potatoes cooked over a campfire grill. Marinate the chicken (or leave it plain), and cut it to serving size before you leave for camp. Place it on the grill and turn it frequently. At home, cut and wash beets, potatoes, carrots, or another family favorite into bite-size pieces, wrap them in foil, and put in a dash of olive oil and water. When you have your coals ready for grilling the chicken, gently place the foil package of veggies in the coals. Turn frequently. You can also steam vegetables by placing them in a pan with water on the grill. The pan will get soot on the bottom, but you will have delicious veggies without firing up your camp stove. If your kids don't like chicken, toss on hot dogs for them. Don't forget buns and ketchup.

If you travel with other families, take turns making meals. When we go for a two-night camping trip with another family, my wife and I prepare dinner the first night and the other parents prepare dinner the second night. It makes camp life easier and more fun if you can watch the kids during dinner preparation then sit down to a good meal.

- Resealable one-quart freezer bags for storing leftovers
- Water bottles for drinking—one for everyone with his or her name on it, and bring an extra or two

Other Camp Gear
Here are a few essential camp items that we are never without.

Head Lamp
Everyone needs a light, including the kids. They are essential for reading in the tent, doing camp chores at dusk, and avoiding logs when walking to the toilet after dark. They come in many brands and price ranges. Take care of them, and they will last a while. Younger kids might do better with a cheap flashlight they can hold in their hands and wave around. Bring extra batteries, especially for kids who like to read at night in the tent.

Battery-Powered Fluorescent-Bulb Lantern
Forget about a propane lantern with kids. The mantles are fragile and the lanterns get hot. Get a couple battery-powered lanterns. We use them almost exclusively in the tent or when getting ready for bed. Generally we don't like lighting up our camp at night because part of the fun for my family is to watch stars or sit around a small fire.

Folding Camp Chairs and Roll-Up Table
Camp chairs come in adult and kid sizes and are great for eating meals or sitting around the fire. Most likely, you will have a picnic table at a campground, but not always.

Five-Gallon Water Jug
It's always nice to have extra water for drinking, washing hands, and cleaning up after meals, without having to walk to the campground spigot. I fill it up at home so I don't have to get water when we roll into camp.

Solar Shower
Solar showers are vinyl bags that, when filled with water and set in the sun for a few hours, heat water to a mild temperature. I've had them get as hot as 100 degrees F in a few hours of direct midday sun. They are great for cleaning feet before bed, doing camp dishes, or general washing. We have a small folding wood platform that we can stand on to keep our feet out of the mud. It folds together and makes a nice storage case for soap, shampoo, and the sun shower when it's not in use. If you get hot and sweaty on a bike ride or your kids get covered with beach sand, take a complete shower.

Tarp
It's always good to have a tarp. Any inexpensive vinyl one will do, but preferably one that has grommets in the edges. Get one that's medium size, say ten by twelve feet. You can string it between trees and your car for a rain shelter or shade, or tie it between your car and a tree to serve as a shower curtain.

Cord
Don't forget to bring 100 feet of parachute cord. This lightweight, inexpensive cord can be used to tie up your tarp, string up wet clothing, anchor your tent, or many other things.

Towels
Bring a stack of towels, especially if you're going to the beach, lake, or a campground with a wading stream. If you're tight on space, bring several small towels and leave the giant beach towels at home. Chances are, once they are wet, they won't dry out, so multiple smaller towels are better than a few large towels.

Packing the Whole Shebang
The first car camping trip ever or even the first trip of the season takes a bit of time to get ready for. All your gear is in storage around the garage. Take some time to assemble your gear a week or two in advance of your first trip of the season. Once packed, keep it ready to go so you don't have to spend too much time packing when you have a free weekend. My strategy is to use four plastic boxes for all our gear, which stay packed and fully stocked all summer. When we return from a trip, we clean items and restock things. Then we can be ready to go camping in a few hours' notice.

First, most of our camping gear stores in two large forty-gallon plastic Action Packer boxes by Rubbermaid. These are heavy-duty, waterproof, lockable boxes. In one box we keep all the kitchen stuff for camping: everything from our solar shower to cook set and stove. After a trip, we clean all the dishes, wash the towels, and restock the items we used. In a second box we have four sleeping bags and sleeping pads. There's usually not room for the tents, camp chairs, or folding table.

Our food goes into two containers. The dried goods are packed in a clear plastic box so we can see through it. Generally once it's packed in the spring, it stays full all summer with nonperishable items like pancake mix, oatmeal, crackers, canned tuna, granola bars, cereal, and the like. Before a trip we add items that are perishable like bread, chips, and s'more supplies.

Finally, we have an omnipresent red cooler that gets packed the day we

How Kids Can Help

Involve your kids in all aspects of camping. It will be more enjoyable for you, and they will have a ball. Here's how my kids help.

- We make a grocery list together and then go to the store the day before our trip. We have a ball cruising the aisles for camp food, especially treats.
- We get out the camp gear together. My daughters insist on testing their sleeping bags on the front lawn. Sometimes we even set up a play tent the week before.
- We gather all the gear and load the car. I go through a mental checklist out loud ("Bikes?" "Check!" yell my daughters, and so on for fifteen minutes).
- We pack, or rather clean out, the car toy box to make sure we have crayons, art supplies, books, and other activities for the drive.
- We pack clothing the night before, although I have to closely supervise this, or they end up with four or five dresses and a half-dozen unmatched pajamas for a two-night trip.

leave with milk and other perishables. I'm not a big fan of filling the cooler with crushed ice or blocks of ice. The ice melts and the cooler becomes a swamp. Nor do those little freezer packets keep food cold for multiday trips. Here is my secret: Every spring I fill four plastic half-gallon jugs, the kind that milk or orange juice comes in, with water. I put these in the freezer so they become solid blocks of ice. Then when we head out on a trip, I use these frozen ice jugs to keep our milk, yogurt, cheese, and drinks cold. When nestled among the food, they last up to a week. The bonus is that there's no mess in the cooler when the ice melts. Plus, when we return home, they go back in the freezer for the next trip. There's nothing worse than a swampy cooler full of half melted ice mixed with spilled milk and bits of bread.

A camping storage system makes it easy to get ready and go camping. The more time and effort it takes preparing to go, the more difficult it becomes to get motivated. The truth is, we can get ready in a few short hours, often quicker than some of our friends with self-contained RVs.

PLANNING A TRIP

Planning a trip can be fun and exciting. You want a trip that is easy when you are first starting out. You should be able to roll into camp and find your

For a midday rest, find some shade.

campsite without too much worry or hassle. We tend to return time and again to our favorite local spots, but we also like to try a few new campgrounds or parks every summer. Here are some tips for planning a trip.

First, choose a state, county, national park, or national forest campground. Many private campgrounds are nice too. Some campgrounds have full bathrooms including toilets, showers, and sinks. Other more basic campgrounds have pit or self-composting toilets and a spigot for obtaining drinking water. For my pro-camping kids, it doesn't matter. But if you are new to camping, there's nothing wrong with seeking out a campground with hot showers and flush toilets. If this is what a family member needs for an enjoyable trip, go for it.

If you can, reserve a site in advance. For busy places in midsummer, this might mean planning several months ahead. With kids, especially young ones, you need to know you have a spot reserved, especially if you drive for some distance. It is not fun to drive two hours on Friday evening to find the campground full. This is more of a problem with popular state campgrounds or national parks, especially those with RV hookups. Some of our local primitive national forest campgrounds always have open spots, even on Fourth of July weekend.

Go somewhere close to home when starting out. You don't need to drive for a whole day to have loads of fun. Try the closest campground to your house. I love it when we can get away for one night and we only have to drive half an hour. This is easy for the kids. And if you have to abort the trip for any reason, home is close-by. We can even be home by noon the next day.

If the weather is nasty, if your kids are a bit ill, or something isn't right, don't go. It's not worth forcing the issue. At the same time, know that the first trip is the hardest one. The second go-round is much easier. By the end of the summer, your system will be down pat, and your kids will even help.

SETTING UP CAMP

We don't spend a ton of time setting up camp right when we roll into the campground. When we get to our spot, the kids want to explore the place on foot or on bikes. Sometimes, they want to head right to the beach if we're on the coast. If the weather is good and we have plenty of daylight, we spend some time exploring or biking. If it is late in the day or the weather looks marginal, we set up the tent first at least. Remember, the more elaborate your camp, the more difficult it is to set up and break down. Keep things simple. I forgo the fancy tarp shelters and elaborate camp kitchens.

Many campsites have a designated tent plot. If not, choose one that is level and protected from wind. Situate your tent so the door is downwind and you have easy access to it. Keep in mind that you want your tent out of the main flow of foot traffic around camp. You don't want the kids tripping or riding bikes over guy lines. I almost always set up the rain fly too, unless it's a hot, sunny midsummer trip. You'll stay dry and warm with the fly.

Our camp kitchen is self-contained in our chuck box as described above. Usually we set up the kitchen on a picnic table. Remember to keep the stove at one end, away from where young kids might be eating. Also, we try not to unload all the food boxes from the car but rather pack them so they are easily accessible from the car. By keeping the food in the car, we have less to load up when we leave, and we don't worry about small critters getting into our food. When packing, think about what you need to unpack first when you arrive in camp and what items or boxes will stay in the car. Bikes, tent, sleeping bags, camp chairs, and toys should be readily accessible.

You will probably have easy access to bathrooms if you're in a campground, but you might want to set up your solar shower, which can double as a hand- or dish-washing station. We usually put ours on the roof of our car. By opening one door and stringing a tarp between the car and a tree, we have a simple private shower.

Remember, you can make your camp kid-safe by paying attention to the general layout. Keep the tent, car, and bikes away from the fire. Make sure your kids know the boundaries of your campsite and how far they can

Snack and rest time at camp.

go without you. Build a campfire only in the designated pit and only if an adult supervisor will be there the whole time. Remember, since kids are generally not used to outdoor fires at home, they will be fascinated with it. They can easily burn themselves by playing with sticks, poking the fire, touching hot stones, or similar mishaps.

Keep a fire small. You don't need a roaring blaze to roast marshmallows or make s'mores. Plus, if a fire is too big, you just burn all your wood too fast and you won't be able to sit near it. Keep a campfire small, tidy, and in the pit. Kids should have cotton pajamas if they like to sit by the fire in their pjs before bed. Polyester pajamas are more flammable.

STUFF TO DO

Most of the time when you go camping you won't really need to plan activities. Kids love exploring, hiking, riding bikes around camp, socializing with other campground kids, and playing at the beach. Make sure you are with them at all times. Kids won't be used to hazards like logs, streams,

Car Camping Safety

Here is a quick memory jogger for setting up camp.

- With young kids, choose a safe campsite with minimal rocks, sticks, or stumps in the main camping area.
- Be careful with fire. Always supervise your kids.
- Watch for cars if you are biking, walking, or playing near the campground road.
- Be prepared for foul weather.
- Keep kitchen gear stowed when not in use.
- Set up your tent away from foot or bike traffic.

stumps, noxious plants, dangerous animals, and the like. One reason we like going to the same campground in the summer (and many times the same tent site) is that my younger kids become familiar with it.

Use the campground as a base camp for day outings such as hikes, bike rides, beach play, or sightseeing.

Don't forget to bring bikes. Most campgrounds are bike central for all ages of kids, especially school-age and preteen kids. Bring a few outdoor activities like a soccer ball, football, baseball gear, or a Frisbee. It's nice to have a few activities for rainy tent-bound days too. Young kids will need crayons, art pens and pencils, puzzles, and reading books. Older kids may like books, a journal, a deck of cards, arts and crafts supplies, and a CD or MP3 player.

Don't forget special treats and camp activities like roasting marshmallows and making s'mores or building sand castles on the beach.

Also your kids, especially if they are older, should help with camp chores: collecting firewood, cleaning dishes, getting water, and setting up the tent.

7

Backpacking

Backpacking is a special time for families. You hike into the wilderness with all your supplies on your back in one of the simplest, most meaningful times with your kids. Younger kids will be awed and fascinated by the beautiful waterfalls, soothing streams, wonderful meadows, or rugged mountains. Look for wildlife, try to identify birds or flowers, or watch stars at night. For families with older kids, this is a magical time: no telephone, television, or computer. Talk, laugh, set up camp, cook, and share a tent with your kids. Watch the sunset, drop a line in the lake to catch dinner, or explore.

In some respects, planning is a bit more tedious when compared with car camping. You'll have less gear, and you need to plan food more precisely. As a parent, you may be carrying the bulk of the food, the cook set, and the tent. Your pack will be heavy. The older your kids get, the more they can carry themselves.

My friends Joel and Julie went backpacking for the first time when their kids were six and four. They picked an easy trail that was only two miles from car to camp. They hiked in slowly. Julie had an eye on the kids, and Joel had a huge pack with the tent, food, and cooking gear. It was a long way in. But once at June Lake, they had a ball. Joel's pack was so heavy that the next morning he made two trips to the car. He made one trip with the tent, sleeping bags, and cooking gear, while Julie played with the kids at the lake. Then he came back to the campsite, and they all hiked out together, Joel and Julie with much lighter packs.

Do a shakedown trip for your first outing. A shakedown is a practice trip that is close to home and close to the car. Try a trip that is only a few miles from your car on a trail you know well (in other words, pick a trail you've hiked on a day trip in the recent past). If you have problems, you can easily make it to your car at any time of day or night, especially if you know the trail and your car is nearby.

GEARING UP
You can't take loads of food and clothing when backpacking. You have to be specific when you pack and make sure your pack isn't too heavy. In fact, one of the great joys of backpacking is the simplicity. When I go on trips, I tend to focus on the light-is-right principle. It means the lighter your pack, the easier it is to hike and the more fun you have. I tend to be a minimalist; I take the minimum I need for a safe, comfortable trip. With kids, that's doubly important since I'm hauling their gear too. Here's the lowdown on equipment.

Backpack
You'll need a large pack for backpacking. For parents, a 3,500-cubic-inch pack is the bare minimum. You'll probably prefer one that is 4,000 to 5,000 cubic inches so you have room for your family gear. Kids should take a pack that fits them well, and it should be loaded with whatever they can comfort-

---

Backpacking Gear

- Backpack
- Socks, underwear, long underwear, cotton or synthetic shirt, shorts, pants
- Raincoat or warm coat, fleece sweater or jacket, fleece vest, hat, gloves, extra socks
- Boots for hiking, camp shoes like sport sandals
- Food for breakfast, snacks, lunch, and a hot meal for dinner
- Camp stove, cook pot, potholder
- Personal eating utensils: spoon, bowl, cup
- Water bottle or hydration bladder system
- Personal toiletries
- Tent
- Sleeping bag and pad
- Activities
- First aid and emergency kit
- Toys, art kits, or books

Canyoneering kid style: cool water hiking in the hot summer.

ably carry. Age, size, physical condition, and enthusiasm all play a role in how big and how heavy each kid's pack should be. A small nine-year-old may take a small pack with clothing and a sleeping bag. An older teen may want to carry his or her own share of the food and cooking gear. As a parent, you should be prepared to take more than your share of the gear, no matter what your kid's age. Don't stress about this, just do it. If it's too much for you, wait to go backpacking until your kids are older and stronger and can carry much of their own gear as well as group items like the stove and tent.

Size and fit of the pack are important. Have your local camping store fit a pack to you and your child. Frame size and pack style are variable. Most people will choose internal frame packs since they are lighter and smaller. However, external frame packs can be very comfortable, especially when loaded down with extra gear. And sometimes they are less expensive.

Pay attention to how you load your backpack. Put your bulky sleeping bag and spare clothing at the bottom. Put heavy items like the cookstove and food close to your lower back. Light things and items you will need on the trail (water, rain jacket, and trail snacks) go near the top for easy access. Some packs have easy-access pockets for trail food or water-bottle holsters.

Food
Food for backpacking will depend on your family's tastes. Most people abide by the following routine: no-cook or instant breakfast, snack all day, then one dinner meal that you cook on your camp stove. That said, some people with smaller kids may prefer to plan an organized lunch. This way, everyone gets a break and you make sure your kids eat. See the sidebar for my typical food list. Above all, keep pack food simple, nutritious, and familiar.

Water
Water is important. You need to make sure that you and your kids drink. Also, keep in mind that the water should be purified as noted in chapter 2.

Sample Backpacking Menu

Breakfast
- Bagels with cream cheese or peanut butter
- Instant oatmeal
- Cold cereal with powdered milk

Lunch and Snacks
- Trail mix
- Granola or energy bars
- Dried fruit
- String cheese
- Peanut butter and jelly sandwiches
- Salami
- Cheese slices
- Crackers
- Fruit leather
- Peanut butter crackers

Dinner
- Pasta with sauce and bagels
- Prepackaged freeze-dried dinner
- Turkey sandwich
- Burritos (reheat precooked beans, rice, veggies)

One way to take water is to use water bottles. Bike bottles work great for kids, since they can drink as they hike, and many packs have holsters for easy access to bottles. The bottles are easy to fill and hard to puncture, plus they are spill-proof. The second option is a hydration bladder with a tube. These are common among adults and older kids. They allow you to continually drink from the hose when the bladder is in your backpack. It's nice for parents to have one so kids can drink from the tube, which is basically a long flexible straw. However, you don't want to puncture the bladder, or your whole pack will get soaked. Some packs have internal sleeves specifically to hold water bladders.

Clothing

Appropriate backpack clothing is also vital. Generally you will want to avoid cotton; when it gets wet it doesn't stay warm. The exception is backpacking in the hot desert, where a cotton T-shirt can keep you and your child cooler. On short trips, one change of clothing is probably adequate. Don't forget a fleece sweater, dry socks, a hat and gloves for kids. Even during midsummer, the nights get cool in the woods. Also, bring either a warm jacket or a raincoat.

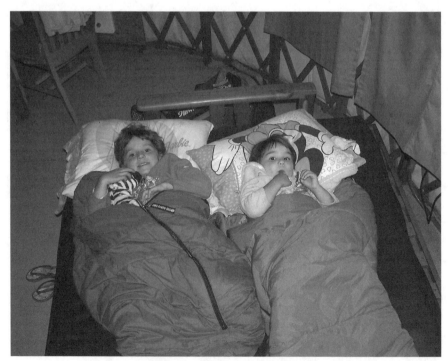

It's all fun, bedding down in a yurt.

Footwear

Good backpacking boots are available from a wide variety of companies in many styles and materials. They are readily available in kids' sizes too. In general, you probably want mid- or high-top boots that are either synthetic cloth or leather. Leather shoes are more durable and more weatherproof. Synthetic boots breathe better and are less expensive. Don't skimp on socks. The best are wool blend, which are durable and warm when wet. Also, it's nice to have some camp shoes for kids, such as sport sandals or inexpensive canvas sneakers.

Tent

A lightweight freestanding dome tent is best for backpacking (see the discussion on tents in chapter 6 for more details). You'll want one big enough for your family plus a vestibule to store packs in case of rain. If you have a large family, consider two smaller tents, which can be lighter. If your kids are older, you can split up the tent, rain fly, and poles to share the load. With younger kids, you are pretty much on your own and must carry the whole thing. If it's midsummer and the weather is hot, consider leaving the rain fly at home for a lighter package.

Sleeping Bag and Pad

Sleeping bags and pads are discussed in chapter 6. It's important that everyone has a quality sleeping bag. For cool nights, have kids wear long underwear to bed instead of pjs and a sweater or hat for extra warmth.

Cooking Gear

Your cooking kit will be much smaller and simpler for backpacking when compared with car camping. Generally you'll bring a basic one-burner backpacker's stove. There are several types of stoves based on the type of fuel they burn: white gas and butane are the most common. I like butane stoves when out with kids. There's no mess like there is with white gas, and butane burns clean. It gets very hot, too, so water boils quickly. The only downside is you have to buy prefilled canisters that are not refillable (they can be recycled, though). White gas, also known as Coleman fuel, is a refined type of gasoline. The canisters have to be filled before use. Because you have to pump the fuel bottle and then prime the stove, it can be a bit messy and more time consuming.

Your basic cook set will probably include just one or two pots. If you're like me and want to keep meals simple, you'll plan one-pot dinners when backpacking. In other words, everything gets cooked or reheated in one pot so you minimize the time it takes to cook and clean up. Usually everyone will carry their personal eating set: a spoon, a bowl, and a cup made from plastic. You can probably forgo plates.

Toiletries

For backpacking, hygiene is still very important. You shouldn't let hand washing slip, nor should you forget a toothbrush. Bring toothbrush, dental floss, toothpaste, toilet paper, liquid soap, wet wipes, and a waterless alcohol-based hand cleanser. Make sure everything is travel-size and in spill-proof containers. Don't forget sunscreen.

Activities

You might want to bring along one or two activities that are small and light-weight. It's nice to have some quiet time in camp. Worst case scenario, you wake in the morning to a downpour. Older kids will like to bring a journal, a book, a deck of cards, or perhaps a CD or MP3 player (although this adds weight). Younger kids will have fun with crayons, a favorite book, a small doll, a toy truck, or a stuffed animal.

PLANNING A TRIP

There are backpacking trails and campgrounds in every state. Some trails are short and flat. Others are long and strenuous. Wherever you live, you can probably find a trail to hike that is suitable for families. Part of planning a trip depends on the ages of your kids, the physical condition of your family, your outdoor experience, and your motivation. Take some time and research trips. Read a guidebook of backpack trips in your area. Talk it over with experts at your backpacking supply store. Ask friends for tips on trails that work well for kids. Call the local rangers for trip ideas and trail conditions.

Look for trails in national or state parks, national or state forests, wilderness areas, or other public areas with designated hiking trails. You can choose loop hikes or trails that take you out to a camp spot then back to your car on the same trail. Out-and-back trails are better for your first trips with kids since you can turn around at any time if you have a problem. Loop hikes can be fun and adventurous, though, since you see new terrain during your whole trip.

You can plan on hiking somewhere between one and four miles per hour. It's best to plan to go one or two miles per hour, and hike somewhere between two and six hours per day, depending on the ages of your kids. For young kids, the best backpacking trips are those that are close to the car. Our standard first trip in my area is the two-mile trail to June Lake in the Mount Saint Helens National Volcano Monument. Remember, the fun is in

Helpful Tips for Backpacking

- A small foam pad is great to sit on while in camp.
- Extra camp shoes, such as lightweight tennis shoes or sport sandals, allow your feet to rest from hiking boots.
- An empty collapsible water bottle or bladder is great for storing extra water in camp.
- Bring an extra warm sleeping bag and a rain- and wind-proof tent so you don't have to bring so many clothes.
- Choose a nice pack. Don't skimp, especially if you are carrying most of the gear.
- Bring an extra sweater, a dry pair of socks, a hat, and gloves, for any season. Make sure the kids have them too.
- Long underwear adds extra warmth at night or when hiking.
- Don't forget sunscreen and a sun hat.

the journey, not necessarily the goal, distance, or difficulty. Start with short trips and build up to longer trips over the summer and over the years.

In busy seasons and popular spots, you may have to get reservations. Call ahead to reserve a backcountry campsite and hiking permit if necessary. Always check the weather too. You don't want to be surprised by a storm that was predicted a day or two in advance. Check with the ranger for any specific trail hazards such as washouts, bear sightings, or high water. Find out if rangers monitor the FRS radio channel and if cell phones work. For prolonged trips in remote areas, consider renting a satellite phone for emergencies. Most cities have satellite phone rental companies, or you can check the internet. A friend who hiked for five weeks with her three kids on the Pacific Crest Trail brought one along for emergencies but never had to use it. I took one on my last extended trip to Baja and was amazed at how well it worked and how inexpensive it was.

Don't forget plenty of patience and a flexible attitude. It will be difficult packing and planning during your first few outings. But once you go on two or three trips, it will be much easier and much more fun.

ON THE TRAIL

Once you've planned a trip and driven to the trailhead, you're ready to head out with your family.

Hiking pace will vary between families, and you should hike only as fast as your slowest member. Don't make anyone stressed or anxious by

Kids are fascinated with every rock, so take your time.

leaving them in the dust. Remember, the fun is in the journey, not how many miles you can cover. It's best to stay together and take regular breaks. Don't worry if it takes you half a day to get two miles to your campground.

Be attentive for blisters. Stop if someone has a sore spot on his or her foot before a blister forms. Usually you can apply moleskin or tape to prevent a full-blown blister. Also, make sure boots are laced properly and change into clean, dry socks if needed.

Remember to take regular breaks for water, food, and rests. You might choose to stop every twenty minutes with young kids or every hour with teenagers. Stop in a sunny spot or where you have logs or rocks to sit on. Take off your packs, eat a bit, and drink some water. Take time to remove layers of clothing if it's warm. If the weather is cool, put on a jacket while you are taking a break so you retain body heat. Don't wait until your kids get cold to make them add a layer.

When hiking, watch for obstacles on the trail. Downed logs or large boulders can be slick. Trails can be muddy. Talus or scree slopes can be loose

Backpacking Safety

Like hiking and car camping, there are numerous safety tips for backpacking that you and your kids should follow. They will help keep you out of trouble.

- Stay on the trail and camp in designated tent sites.
- Bring extra food, water, clothing, and a small emergency kit.
- Let someone know your plan.
- Bring a map and compass (and know how to use them).
- Stay together when hiking.
- Take regular breaks for rest, food, and water.
- Carry an FRS radio, cell phone, or satellite phone for emergencies.
- Watch animals from a distance.
- Store your food properly.

and uneven. Watch for swift streams, especially if you have to cross a stream via logs or rocks. Most developed trails use bridges for stream crossings of any significance.

SETTING UP CAMP

Once you've made it to your campsite, set up your camp. It's best to set up your tent and kitchen area before nightfall or foul weather sets in. Find a flat spot for your tent. Try not to clear too many logs or rocks—remember Leave No Trace. Most campsites, even primitive ones, have an obvious tent site.

Unfurl your sleeping pad and bag in the tent, and then zip the tent closed. And keep it closed. You don't want bugs or dirt getting in the tent.

Set up your food area and kitchen spot. When backpacking, you'll probably have just a small stove and small cook set. Find a flat rock or smooth area in the dirt away from the tent. After you cook, you'll need to store all the food. The best option is to hang it in a tree away from your tents so animals won't get to it or be drawn to your tents. If you are in bear country, you'll need to take additional steps to keep it safe according to the campground rules and guidelines. Some areas have bear poles, high poles with a crossbar and a rope to string up your food cache. Some bear-area camps have designated kitchen spots well removed from the tent sites.

Once your tent and camp kitchen are set up, you'll probably need to get water from a stream. Make sure you purify it as noted in the sidebar in chapter 2. Get enough water for the evening meal and for breakfast the next morning. It's nice if you can fill up everyone's water bottles for the next day's hike too. I often carry an empty collapsible water bladder for camp water.

Don't forget, once you finish cooking, clean all the dishes and scatter dishwater and food scraps over a broad area away from the tents and water source.

You may be in a campsite with a primitive toilet, outhouse, or latrine. If not, bury human waste in a small hole about six to eight inches deep at least three hundred feet from water. You can bury toilet paper, but some people pack it out because small animals will dig it up. Remember to wash hands after going to the bathroom and before meals.

Biking

Biking is one of the most popular and ubiquitous activities for families. Nearly every kid has a bike. If you've ever been to a state or national park campground in the summer, you've seen bike central firsthand. For younger kids, biking at campgrounds or on bike paths is a staple outdoor activity. Older kids will love mountain biking on forest single tracks, on beach sand, or on dirt roads. Biking is versatile, loads of fun, and anyone can do it. Plus it is a great activity for mixed families or for families who have kids separated by a large age range. Everyone has their own bike and, within limits, can ride at their own pace. Grandma and grandpa can go along, and a tandem provides loads of laughs and bonding time.

Even before your kids start riding their own bikes, you can take them along on bike trips. My kids started out riding in the kid seat that attaches to my bike. This plastic seat sits above the rear wheel on a rack. I could interact with my kids: I'd point out squirrels and chipmunks, or sometimes we'd sing. When I had two kids, my children liked riding in the bike trailer, a kid carrier on wheels that is pulled behind my bike. It's like a rolling play pen. But neither the bike seat nor trailer lasted more than a year or two. Before long, they were riding their own bikes and the tandem trailer bike (described below).

One of our favorite camping trips is a bike trip. We load up our car, the Gorilla, gather some friends, and head out to Lower Falls Camp on the Northwest's famous Lewis River Trail. The campground has biking for all ages, and families with kids ranging from infants to teenagers typically join us. For the little kids, a paved campground loop is perfect for riding endless circles. For the older kids, the campground has several single-track bike trails that explore the woods. The trails are narrow but they are soft forest duff and lead through thick groves of old-growth Douglas fir, western red

Dad's getting a workout trail-a-biking.

cedar, and giant hemlock. The paths are flat, with an occasional hill, lots of scenic vistas, and tons of scurrying chipmunks and squirrels.

When my oldest daughter wanted a challenge, I took her on the tandem trailer bike up the single-track trail for an hour's ride. We stopped at a huge waterfall to have a snack, and she loved it. By the time we got back to camp, she was beaming and couldn't wait to ride her own bike around the paved campground loop again. My youngest was so impressed with the tandem trailer bike that she hopped on at age two; we rode it around the paved loop. She too had an ear-to-ear grin. No, that was me with the ear-to-ear grin.

The thing I like about bikes is that everyone has one, almost everyone can ride one to some degree, and bikes are not hugely expensive. This is an excellent activity if grandma and grandpa are in good shape. It is fun for blended, extended, and large families too.

GEARING UP

Buying a bike for your child is actually pretty simple. You will likely find bikes in excellent condition from garage sales or friends whose kids are a bit older than yours. Look for bikes at discount stores or outdoor stores. For young kids, don't spend a bundle. Once your child is a teenager, you can invest in a better bike, since he or she won't outgrow it.

Bikes Sizes

Basically, the key to buying a bike for your child is that he or she should be able to touch the ground when sitting on the seat. The seat is adjustable somewhat, but it's better to have a slightly small bike, especially for school-age kids. You don't have to spend a huge amount of money on a bike. The least expensive bikes usually work fine, especially for younger kids. Little bikes tend to be a bit heavier since many parts are made out of steel, not aluminum or lighter composite materials. And don't be afraid to accessorize. Your kid might love streamers from the handlebars, baskets, handlebar pads, a water bottle cage, or a bell.

Bikes for small kids are sized by the wheels.

- A twelve-inch-wheel bike fits a child from two to five years old with an inseam of roughly thirteen to sixteen inches. This is your child's first bike with training wheels. These bikes are low to the ground and just as stable, if not more so, than a tricycle. Tricycles tend to be wobbly and difficult to turn; in fact, my kids never rode one. They started out on the twelve-inch bike.
- The next step is a sixteen-inch wheel, which will work from ages four through six, or an inseam from sixteen to twenty-two inches. These bikes tend to be the ones kids learn to ride without training wheels. They are easy to ride, and kids don't outgrow them as fast as smaller bikes.
- From age six and up, choose either a twenty- or twenty-four-inch-wheel bike. These bikes are for kids who can ride independently without training wheels. The twenty-inch bike works for shorter, smaller kids. The twenty-four-inch bike will last longer, through teenage years. Some twenty-inch bikes have a coaster break and rear-rim break. These are easy for kids to transition to from sixteen-inch bikes. Other twenty-inch bikes have front and rear brakes, five-speed shifters, and no coaster brakes—these are a bit more challenging to ride but will last kids into their teens.
- Once you child weighs over 100 pounds, you will move into an adult bike. These are usually twenty-six-inch wheels, but in addition, they come in different frame sizes: small, medium, and large. You should probably have them fitted at a bike store because it is more complex.

Getting the Training Wheels Off

You feel a deep satisfaction and pride welling up from your heart and sparking a tiny electrical zip up your spine. You watch her pedal across the vacant parking lot, all on her own. Away she goes, the product of many days of hard work. No parent can forget the feeling of immense love and pleasure from teaching children to ride without training wheels.

I remember when my oldest daughter Skylar rode her bike without training wheels for the first time. We tried a few times earlier in the year, but she wasn't ready. I kept reminding her on a regular basis that I'd be happy to help her try, but she wasn't ready. Several months later, after watching two neighbor kids attempt the challenge, Skylar said, "Papa, take my training wheels off please."

We tried for an hour a day for a week: at our local park, at the vacant paved lot down by the marina, at the high school track, at the campground where we'd gone that weekend. Working a little bit each day, first I ran with her, both hands on the bike. Then I had one hand on the bike. Then one finger. Then nothing. We made a deal when she didn't want me to let go of the bike: I would let go, but I wouldn't let her fall. She trusted me, and I followed through, even though my back had a massive spasm after an hour of running alongside catching her falls.

Then it happened somewhat suddenly—she rode away with a clean and brisk stroke, pedaling as if she'd done it for a month. She smiled, but I smiled bigger I think. It's a small piece of her childhood but an enormous part of parenting.

Ready to take off the training wheels? Well, first make sure your

Save your money and buy a nice bike for your kids when they are in their early teens. That way, they will keep it for a long time. For teenagers, look for bikes with aluminum wheels, quality components like brakes and derailers (the gadget that shifts the chain), and a frame that is constructed of aluminum. These features make the bike lighter and also last longer.

Helmets

Helmets are a mandatory safety item. When kids are young, it can be difficult to get them to wear one. We followed the strategy of not giving them a choice. In other words, when your kids are young, teach them that a helmet child is ready. Here are some tips to try. Remember, if one thing doesn't work, try something else. All these techniques help kids learn balance. Every kid is different. I've seen some work two weeks and others jump on and ride without training wheels on the first day.

- Move the training wheels up about half an inch. This makes the bike just a bit wobbly.
- Let your child learn to balance on a scooter.
- When you take the training wheels off, hold the seat and run beside her.
- As she learns to balance, move your hand to supporting her back. Alternatively, hold her jacket or shirt.
- Some kids prefer wearing knee and elbow pads and gloves. That way, if they fall, they minimize injury. This can really boost their confidence.
- Practice on flat ground, preferably soft areas. Our favorite practice spot was the high school track. It is flat, wide open, and the rubberized surface is much more forgiving than asphalt.
- Practice at short spurts. An hour or five minutes, let your child tell you how much she wants to practice.
- Don't push it. If your child isn't ready, wait.
- Have older kids or peers encourage your child. This is a great confidence booster.
- Ride with other kids in the neighborhood who are learning to ride without training wheels.
- Above all, stay tuned to your child's fear and anxiety.

is part of bike riding and that they can't bike ride without one. Once they get used to wearing a helmet, they won't think twice about it. Most helmets meet Consumer Product Safety Commission (CPSC) or American Society of Testing and Materials (ASTM) standards. Usually a sticker on the helmet denotes that it meets CPSC or ASTM requirements.

How you fit a helmet on your child is important. Make sure the helmet is snug but comfortable. It shouldn't be too tight that it feels bad or too loose that it slides around the head. The rim should make contact with your child's head in the front, back, and both sides. When it sits on your child's head, the helmet should be level and cover the forehead within two fingers of his or her eyebrow. Many helmets come with pads to improve fit and comfort. The strap should be snug, and your child shouldn't be able to remove the helmet without undoing the strap. Be careful you don't pinch his or her chin when you put the strap on!

Once your child has the helmet on, do this test: Have him or her make a big yawn to open the mouth wide. The helmet should pull down tightly on the head. If it doesn't, the chin strap is probably too loose. Also, see if the helmet rocks back and forth on the head. You might need to adjust the straps if it does.

Ventilation is good in helmets for kids, especially if you live in a warm climate or your child is older. Removable sweat bands and pads are nice so you can wash them. Kids love bright colors, and you can see them better.

Don't forget, if your child does have a significant fall or you notice damage, replace the helmet. Helmets are good for only one crash and can wear over time, especially with lots of sun exposure, which breaks down plastics.

Clothing

Young kids can ride bikes in any pair of shorts and a T-shirt. But when your kids get older and start doing longer rides, they may want some bike-specific clothing. Bike shorts are specially designed from stretchy Lycra with a thick pad to protect the bottom. These allow free motion of pedaling without chafing of the thighs or making a sore bum. For shirts, a synthetic polypropylene shirt will keep your kids the warmest on cool days. A bike-specific wind- or raincoat is nice because it usually has a long tail for covering your bottom when riding and a rear pocket for snacks.

Gloves

Gloves are important for biking. Kids don't really need them to prevent blisters, but they do protect their hands if they fall. This is important on a campground road or a trail. Kids normally stretch out a hand or arm when they fall, and they can easily cut their hands if they land on a rock or stick.

Pad Kits

You can buy pad kits for kids who bike, which usually include elbow and knee pads and gloves. They are nice because they double as skate, scooter, or rollerblade pads. Some kids love them, some will never wear them.

You're probably thinking, "When I was a kid, I never wore bike pads." And that's a great point. Some experts think it's good for a child to learn how to fall and that they can get hurt. You don't want kids to think they are invincible. A few scratches never hurt any child. Also, once some kids get

Tips for Getting Your Child to Wear a Helmet

If you need tips on getting your young children to wear a helmet, try the following. Remember, don't let your kids wear a bike helmet when at a playground or doing other activities. They can catch it on a tree or swing.

- Start early with a helmet, so your children learn that it is a mandatory part of biking.
- Focus on the fun of biking, not the helmet.
- Make a game out of it—wear it at home first. Let them walk around with it or play dress-up with it.
- Let them pick out the helmet color. Let them customize it with stickers.
- Make a big deal, even reward your children with a sticker or small toy, when they wear their helmets without whining.
- Show them big kids who wear helmets.
- Make sure everyone is wearing a helmet. This means you too.
- Look for a child-oriented safety book or coloring book that discusses bike safety. You might find this at your library or local bike store.

used to wearing pads, they may not want to go biking without them. We have one friend whose child won't get on his bike unless he has a helmet, knee pads, elbow pads, and gloves.

On the other hand, pads can be fun, and they can eliminate some of the parent's and kid's anxiety of learning to bike. We found that pads were most useful when our kids were learning to ride without training wheels and when biking on dirt trails for the first time.

Eye Protection

Don't forget eyewear. Sunglasses are important for sun protection and to guard against flying debris, tree limbs, or flying insects, especially when trail biking.

Water and Food

You'll need water and a snack when biking. Most bikes come with a water bottle cage or brackets to mount one. These wire or plastic cages hold a bike-specific water bottle that can easily be accessed when riding. Another option is a small backpack with a hydration bladder. These biking-specific backpacks have a vinyl water bladder and a long hose. The hose wraps around the pack to the front straps. This allows you or your child to drink from the hose while biking. This is a great option to keep kids drinking and is easier to use than a water bottle. There are many brands of hydration backpacks, and some are available in kids' sizes. Bike backpacks also have room for a rain jacket and a snack.

Repair Kit

Everyone should bring a repair kit for bikes, except perhaps young kids. This is great for teenagers, since they should learn to repair their own bikes when dad isn't around. You can stuff repair tools in your backpack. Alternatively, get a small pouch that fits under the bike seat and leave it attached to the bike at all times. That way, you will never be without it. The basic tools include items to change a flat tire. You will need tire irons to get the tire off the rim and either a new inner tube or a patch kit. I bring both—if I use the inner tube for one flat, I have the patch kit for a second flat. The other reason to bring a patch kit is you may not have a tube to fit the smaller tube of a kid's bike. It's also nice to have a small bike tool, which includes a flat and Phillips screwdriver and a set of hex wrenches. These bike-specific tools can tighten most parts on a bike.

Practice changing a flat tire at home first, and make your teens change a tire before they head out on their own. This five-minute chore seems difficult before you actually do it. It's not a matter of if your child will get a flat but when. Flat tires are part of biking. Once kids learn how to change a flat, they realize it's pretty easy.

Make sure your bike is in excellent working condition before you head out. Oil the chain and lubricate pedals, shifters, and brakes if necessary. Clean everything after a ride. Replace worn items frequently, especially brake pads. Remember, a new bike needs to be adjusted after the first few rides. The cables tend to stretch.

BIKING WITH YOUNG KIDS

You have several options besides regular bikes if your children are small. Choose bike trailers, rear seats, or tandem trailer bikes. These allow families to go on longer rides when kids are too young to ride without training wheels or too young to go very far. They are great for riding along a bike path in a campground, around town when vacationing, or at home. They are safe for the most part, but I'd recommend staying well clear of cars, since they are not very maneuverable. Choose a bike path or wide road that is closed to cars.

Child-Carry Bike Trailers

Many parents start out biking with kid bike trailers. These two-wheel trailers attach to the rear of a parent's bike and are towed. Many kids like these, since they can sit in the enclosed portable playground and play with toys, eat snacks, or sleep. They can look around but are protected from the elements, usually with a clear vinyl rain, bug, and rock shield. Most models have a basic roll cage too. For the most part, because they are wide and low, trailers are stable and easy for parents to tow. Most have either a three- or five-point harness, and many can accommodate two kids plus a diaper bag. They are more difficult to squeeze in your car, but luckily, most brands collapse or fold for storage.

Unfortunately, trailers don't work well with helmets; the back rests tend to push children's heads forward and chins down into very awkward positions. And because they ride low and usually have a canopy, your kids' visibility is limited. This can be a bit frustrating if they want to watch for animals or flowers. Also, because kids are enclosed in the trailer and behind the parent's bike, you can't interact with them very well.

When riding, you won't be able to make quick movements. And it is more difficult to pass another biker when on a narrow path or road because of the girth of the trailer.

I'd recommend trying one first. Many shops that rent bikes often rent bike trailers. They connect quickly and simply to almost any bike, except rear suspension frames that have odd designs.

Rear Seats

Rear seats are another option to take your young child on a longer ride. These plastic seats are available at almost any bike shop or retail store with a sports section. They bolt to a rear rack on the parent's bike, and then your child is strapped in. My oldest child didn't like the seat too much, because it was too wobbly. But my youngest loved it because she could participate in the rides with the rest of the family. She sat up high and had a clear view of the scenery. Many parents like these better than trailers. They are less expensive for starters. Plus, because your child will be high, open, and right behind you, you can point out birds and flowers, and he or she can see everything that's going on. Unlike trailers, though, they carry only one child.

I recommend looking for a bike seat with a full cage. The protective plastic should come higher than your child's head and wrap around to the sides to protect the knees and shoulders in a fall. And they should have footrests to keep the child's feet out of the rear wheel spokes.

Because they attach to your bike, these take more skill on the parent's part than a bike trailer. First, you have to balance your bike against your body when loading your kid (you can't use the kickstand). Then you have to ride with an extra weight over your back wheel. The center of gravity is shifted up and back. For parents who are not good bikers, this can be unstable. And you don't want to fall. Even if your bike just tips over, your little guy can get hurt.

Tandem Trailer Bikes

When your kids are older, tandem trailer bikes are a fantastic way to enjoy biking. A tandem trailer bike is a way of turning your bike into a tandem so you and your child can ride together. The trailer bike itself looks like a kid's bike, except there is no front wheel. In its place is a bar that connects to the seat post of a parent's bike. Thus, once connected, you have a tandem bike: the parent's bike plus the trailer bike.

These can be a great transition for kids. My kids loved the trailer bike for the two summers before they could bike without training wheels. The trailer bike pedals just like a regular bike, and you can actually feel it. "Hill coming, pedal!" is what I yell to get my kids to give me a boost. When my kids get tired, they stop pedaling and look for rabbits or squirrels while I do all the work. My kids started this as soon as they were old enough to hold on and pedal by themselves, around age three. We have had many days biking, ranging from beach bikes on campground bike paths to riding our local bike trail near our house.

The great thing about trailer bikes is that even when your kids are older you can still enjoy a tandem ride. Kids will like this throughout their school-age years. In fact, some companies make double tandem trailer bikes, so one adult can take two kids. In other words, a triple bike. This is great for single parents or when dad has the kids for a day. Adams Trail-a-bike comes with an optional back support and harness for young kids.

Another option is a convertible tandem bike bar like that from Trail-gator. This bar attaches to both your bike and your child's. The bar connects your seat tube to the child's bike and lifts up the child's front wheel to make a tandem bike from the two. These are great because you don't have to bring a separate trailer bike, and your child can either ride tandem with the Trail-gator system or ride his or her bike independently. The Trail-gator collapses out of the way on the parent's bike when not in use. Also, it is less expensive than trailer bikes. The downside of the Trail-gator is that it is not quite as stable as regular tandem trailer bikes.

Bike Trains

Bike trains are something you are more likely to see in an outdoor town, vacation spot, or campground. A bike train is basically a combination of a

Tag-a-long biking is a big workout for parents, and the kids can coast.

tandem trailer bike and child-carry bike trailer. You'll see people riding these with two or three kids: One is old enough to ride the tandem trailer bike that is attached to the parent's bike. Another child (or two) sits in the trailer, which is attached to the trailer bike. Thus you have your bike, the tandem trailer bike, and the child-carry bike trailer in a row.

Bike trains are wobbly, very difficult to slow down and stop, and difficult to mount, dismount, load, and unload. But they can be loads of fun for a single parent and for families with more than two kids. Choose flat, wide, paved, uncrowded bike paths for trains. Avoid hills, streets, and cars. Oh, and get ready for a workout.

Biking is a great camp activity.

MOUNTAIN BIKING

With younger kids, you will likely putz around your local bike trail or campground. But when your kids get older, you will want to start going on longer bike rides. You may have a designated paved or dirt bike trail in your community. Or check nearby state parks or national forests. You probably have the option of three types of trails, from easiest to most difficult. Paved bike trails are the easiest. Try these when you start taking longer rides. Dirt or gravel roads are for more advanced families. Single-track trails, those that are only wide enough for bikes, are more difficult. But don't be shy—many single-track dirt trails are flat, smooth, and easy to ride.

When heading out on a family ride, first make sure everyone has food, water, a basic repair kit, gloves, a helmet, and a windbreaker or extra pullover. Then make sure everyone knows the plan. You might be riding down a trail to a specific spot and then returning home on the same trail. This is usually called an out-and-back ride. Alternatively, you may choose a loop trail. Either way, make sure everyone knows the route and has a map if necessary.

Always stay together. It's no fun to have a flat tire with everyone in your family ahead of you on the trail.

Make sure you take regular breaks for snacks and water. A good estimate is to stop every forty-five minutes for a five-minute break. But if you see a nice view point or a cool waterfall, stop at any time.

Here are some additional tips for biking on single-track trails.

- Use the easiest gear for steep hills. Shift before the pedaling gets difficult.
- Use brakes for a controlled descent down hills. Unlike on roads, you may not be able to see a sudden turn or a root or rock on the trail. Most braking power comes from the front brakes. Avoid locking up the rear brake, as you will skid the tire.
- Watch for roots, rocks, mud, and soft sand or dirt. Inconstant terrain is challenging and fun, but it can be wobbly too.
- Get your bum out of the saddle for difficult sections if needed.

OVERNIGHT TOURS

Overnight mountain biking trips can be a blast for families. First, you can carry much of the gear on your bike racks, and not on your back like with backpacking. Second, you can cover more terrain than with backpacking.

There are a number of styles of overnight biking trips. You can choose to stay on roads and ride between campgrounds or even motels. I have friends who took their families across part of America on bikes. You can use

---

Bike Safety

A few safety tips will go a long way toward preventing mishaps. These are some basic ones.

- Watch for and avoid cars.
- Wear a helmet, gloves, and other protective gear.
- Bring water, food, and extra clothing.
- Carry a basic repair kit, and know how to change a flat tire.
- Stay together.
- Watch for obstacles like roots, rocks, sand, or mud.

gear trailers, small backpacks, or panniers (racks that fit over the rear or front wheel) to carry camping and overnight gear.

Another great way to go is with an outfitter. Bike tours are available all over the U.S. You go with a group, preferably with a family-oriented company, and ride between camps. The guide company usually provides a "sag wagon," or a vehicle to shuttle equipment, clothing, and food. Some companies provide meals too.

Finally, you can design your own backcountry bike tour carrying all your own equipment. Stick to national or state parks or recreation areas that have designated bike trails, established campgrounds, and minimal cars.

9

Skiing and Snowboarding

I learned to ski on Oregon's Mount Hood when I was seven years old and had many ski days with my family growing up. I converted to snowboarding in the early 1980s and exclusively climbed mountains just to snowboard down. After almost a decade off the two planks, I started skiing again with my children. Rediscovering this lost passion with my kids has been pure delight. In fact, my dad dug out my old skis from high school, which bring back fond memories of my childhood.

I taught my young children to ski before snowboarding for several reasons. It's easier for kids to learn to ski than for adults. Thus, I feel they should learn this important mountain skill and outdoor sport when they are young. Snowboarding, on the other hand, is easier for older kids and adults to learn. Although my daughters haven't expressed a desire to snowboard yet, I'm sure it's only a matter of time. When Skylar and Avrie are teenagers, they will do whichever sport they want. Or both.

Skiing and snowboarding are lifelong adventure sports and the passion of thousands of families. These fun and rather safe winter sports can accommodate a wide range of skill levels, so trips to the mountains can be fun for the whole family. And there are ski resorts located across the U.S., easily accessible from most major cities. I will start with skiing first: gear, starting out, and learning. Then I'll discuss snowboarding. And finally, I'll give you some alternatives to both—lower budget, easier sports of sledding, snowshoeing, or cross-country skiing.

WINTER CLOTHING

I still remember my first ski gear. When I was seven years old, I found it under the Christmas tree: bright red skis like Dad's and matching red boots.

Group sports can be a blast, especially on a midwinter's day.

After one year I grew out of the boots. I inherited my sister's, which were the exact same model but a few sizes larger.

All kids should have plenty of warm clothes for the mountains. If they are too lightly dressed, they will get cold quickly. If kids are overbundled, a common mistake, they can get too hot, and their movement might be restricted. It's best to dress your kids as you dress yourself. Kids, like their parents, should dress in layers for skiing and snowboarding. Don't spend a fortune on winter clothing. Your kids will grow out of ski clothes way before the clothes wear out. Use hand-me-downs, trade with your friends, and shop ski swaps or outlet stores.

First, long underwear is the next-to-skin layer. Second, a midlayer should consist of a fleece sweater or vest. A full-zip sweater is much easier to get on and off. Sometimes a pullover works better if your child has a tendency to take off his or her sweater. A lightweight vest is nice for warmer spring days; it also makes a compact extra layer that you can carry in your backpack for emergencies. Third, get a warm snowsuit. There are tons of styles, colors, and brands. You don't need expensive materials like Gore-Tex or lots of accessories like fancy pockets or armpit zippers. Basically, you want an insulated jacket and pants that are both windproof and waterproof.

Usually these are tightly woven nylon shells with synthetic material for insulation. For jackets, an attached hood that can fit over a helmet is a must. It will always be there for a sudden snow- or windstorm. Zip handwarmer pockets are great for snacks or a pocket radio. Make sure the cuffs are elastic or Velcro so they can be tightened over mittens.

I've found that regular pants work better for younger kids and bib overalls are okay for older kids. Bibs are a bit warmer, stay up better, and keep the snow out. Pants, however, are much easier to take off when kids have to go to the bathroom. Another hint: Black pants are great because they match almost any jacket and they hide the dirt and grime well. Buy them big—since they will be pulled over ski boots, they won't drag even if they are a size or two big. That way, you'll get a few seasons' use.

You can also buy a one-piece ski suit for your child; these are like coveralls. Although warmer and often less expensive, I've found that they are less versatile and difficult for our kids to get off when they have to go to the bathroom or head in the lodge for a break.

Winter Sports Tips for Making Life Easier

Here are some tips that helped my family:
- Make sure everyone is healthy, had a good breakfast, and had a good night's sleep.
- Take extra food, water, and clothing, especially extra hats, gloves, and socks.
- Pack your ski bag the night before. When I was a kid, I wore my long underwear to bed the night before so I was ready the minute I woke up.
- Take lots of breaks for water or hot chocolate.
- If the weather is bad, don't go. With young kids, choose sunny days.
- Kids learn by watching. Let them follow you, but go at their pace.
- Always carry snacks and water on the ski hill; keep them in your ski parka or a small backpack.
- Above all, don't push your kids. If they aren't having fun, you risk turning them off to skiing or snowboarding altogether.

Important Acessories

- Hat. Make sure you have an extra one for each child. Also, make sure it fits snugly under the helmet.
- Mittens. Generally, mittens are warmer than gloves. Use retainer clips for younger kids so they don't lose their mittens. Older kids might like gloves because they can grip ski poles or attach snowboard bindings easier.
- Neck gaiter. This is essential to keep the neck and face warm if it is cold or windy.
- Socks. Wool blend are the warmest and most durable. Don't use cotton socks because they are not very warm. Make sure socks can be pulled up above the calf to keep them from sliding down. Generally, if kids have ski boots that fit properly, they shouldn't need two pairs of socks on their feet, but bring a backup pair for after skiing.
- Sunglasses or goggles. Buy kids' goggles that are designed for helmets. This is important to keep wind and snow out of their eyes, but also to protect them from the bright rays of the sun. Almost all sunglasses and goggles provide UV light protection, even the cheaper ones. If the lenses get scratched after a few seasons, buy only a replacement lens, not a whole new pair of goggles.

Stay warm and safe: Insist on a helmet.

- Helmet. This is a must for all kids. In fact, some ski areas require them for kids taking lessons. Make sure the helmet fits snugly and the straps are not too loose around the chin. All helmets, even the inexpensive ones, are adequate for safety. Wear a helmet yourself. It is safer, and you'll have an easier time convincing your child to wear one if you have yours on.
- Sunscreen. The sun in the mountains can be especially dangerous. Not only can kids get sunburned, but the sun can be reflected off the snow and intensified. Apply a thick layer of sunscreen on your child's face and neck before you leave the house and again at mid-day.

Organize, Organize, Organize

Once you get all your ski or snowboard gear, you might find that it gets strewn all over the house in drawers and cubbies. The best organizational tip is to have a dedicated ski backpack for each of your children and have a ski station in your garage or mud room. It's best if each member of your family has his or her own cubby, basket, or shelf. When you come home from a trip, hang up the pants and parkas, lay out the wet hats and gloves, and wash long underwear. When dry and clean, put everything back in its own spot; that way, when you head out the next time, each kid can just dress by her cubby and repack his or her own backpack. With young kids, you will need to help with dressing, but trust me, if you have to hunt all over the house for ski clothing in the morning, you're in for a long day.

It helps to have certain gloves and hats dedicated to skiing. If kids use the same pair for school, they will undoubtedly leave them in the school locker or desk on the day you need them for skiing. Take backup mittens, hats, and socks for your kids: They will lose or forget them. And paste a checklist at the door so you don't forget anything before the drive up to the ski hill.

SKI EQUIPMENT

Choosing equipment can be time-consuming, and it is largely dependent on your child's height, weight, and skill level. Many parents choose to rent the first few times. That way, you don't have to spend a bundle of money, and you can try different sizes. Also, the rental shop expert can help you pick out gear. If you know your child will be skiing for a while, you can buy gear later. A good source for inexpensive ski equipment is your local ski swap. Other families in your community may have ski gear that their kids have outgrown. Also, try a used sporting goods store or even the internet.

Boots

Ski boots should be comfortable and have plenty of room in the toes for warmth. If they are too tight, kids' feet will get cold and their toes will cramp. If they are too loose, it will be difficult for them to ski. If you want to buy them a bit big, it's okay to have your children wear an extra pair of socks. Also, you can use a foam foot bed to take up some space in the shell before they fully grow into the boots. Depending on your children's ages, they will likely wear a two- or three-buckle boot. In general, the more buckles, the better the fit. With used boots, check the liner to make sure it's not torn or too compressed. Over time, the foam liner gets squished and thus loses some of its shape and warmth. Check the buckles for worn parts; these can often be replaced at a ski shop.

Bindings

Bindings should be new or checked annually at a ski shop. If they are rusted or old, the springs might not work. They have a tension setting on toe and heel called DIN. The DIN setting is adjusted based on height, weight, skill level, and age of your child. Don't try to set the bindings yourself. Too loose and your kids' skis will pop off all the time. Too tight and they won't eject when necessary, thus risking serious injury. The ski shop should check the bindings and set the DIN annually. The bindings will need to be adjusted as your child grows and becomes a better skier. Again, if you buy used ski gear or borrow from friends, have a shop go over the bindings to make sure they are working properly.

Skis

Shaped skis make learning much easier than it was in years past. These shorter and fatter skis have a significant sidecut, the hourglass shape of skis. They come in lots of brands and colors. Fortunately, almost all skis nowadays are good quality and durable. There are several formulas you can use to approximate the length of ski your child will need. One guide is that the skis should come up to the armpits of your child. A simpler guide is to start with an estimated length, then change skis if too short or too long. Generally, if the ski is too long, it will be difficult to turn. Thus it's always easier to have them a bit shorter. Length gives flotation over deep snow and speed on hard snow; this is something you're not concerned about when learning.

- Under age five and forty pounds: 80 cm.
- Between five and seven years old and forty to sixty pounds: 90 to 100 cm.
- Between seven and nine years old and sixty to eight pounds: 110 to 120 cm.

- Between ten and twelve and eighty to one hundred pounds: 120 to 130 cm.
- Over age twelve and one hundred pounds: 130 to 150 cm.

One device you will need to teach kids to ski is a tip clip that holds ski tips together. There are several brands, but the one I like best is the Edgie-Wedgie. This six-inch-long elastic tube is attached to each ski tip with a thumb screw. It holds the ski tips together while your child learns to snow-plow.

Poles

Generally, toddlers don't need poles right away. Once they get the hang of the snow-plow, however, poles will help them balance and keep their hands in front of their bodies. Also, it gives them the feeling that they are big-kid skiers. Once they can go down the hill and turn, it's time to get them poles. School-age kids need poles from the get-go, for balance and support. When buying poles, they should be long enough so that when your child holds the pole, his or her elbow is at 90 degrees.

Okay, you have your gear, and you're ready to go. Before you head out skiing for the first time, dress your child in all the ski gear to make sure it fits. It can be challenging to get him or her dressed in the living room, but make it fun. It's better to know a week or two before your first ski day if something doesn't fit. We do this every year in the fall about a week before the high school ski team swap meet, so we have plenty of time to get replacement clothing or equipment that my kids have grown out of.

BASIC SKI SKILLS

The first days on the slope, help your child practice walking in boots and shuffling around on flat snow with skis on. This helps your child get a feel for his or her boots and skis. Take your time. It may take ten minutes, or it may be an hour for a kid to get used to boots and skis. If you're on a ski vacation, consider doing this the night before your first day on the mountain. Make it fun, laugh a lot, and be silly.

Another way to get your child used to skis is to tow him or her around a flat area. Using your pole, put the pole basket between your child's legs. Then you can hold the handle and pull your kid. It will only take a few minutes for your child to get used to the skis, and before long he or she will be roaring with laughter.

You'll have to teach your child how to fall and get up also. Basically, with low-speed falls, kids should just lean over and hit the snow with their bottoms. This is generally the safest way to fall. Try to keep them from falling on outstretched hands. To get up, teach kids to swing the feet down-

Start early, but be prepared to pull when teaching skiing.

hill, and then use hands (or poles) to push off from the snow. If you are having trouble teaching your child, have him or her lie down on the snow without skis on, then tell them to grow like a tree. Little kids may need help for a while; don't worry, they will figure it out eventually. If they don't catch on right away, move on to the next lessons below.

Riding the Lift

You'll be riding the rope tow or chairlift sooner than you think. Even before your children can ski alone, you need to tote them up the hill. For young kids, you have to carry them on the chairlift or hold them between your legs on the rope tow. Make sure you are not carrying anything else so you have both hands free. Keep your food, water, spare clothes, and camera in a backpack. The most difficult part is getting off the lift. You can signal the lift operator by waving to have the lift slowed or even stopped.

Choose a hill that is not crowded, with a wide and gentle slope and few trees. These are usually marked as beginner slopes with a green circle at North American ski resorts (a blue square identifies intermediate slopes, and a black diamond means experts only). Unfortunately, beginner slopes tend to be crowded. If you can, go on a weekday. Or try skiing right when the lifts open for the day or during lunch hour.

Depending on your child, you can start at a beginner hill with either a rope tow or chairlift. It's easier to carry younger kids on the chairlift, where they can sit on your lap. Older kids might want to start at the rope tow, where they will be able to go up on their own.

Going Downhill

When you're ready to teach your children to go downhill, take it slow. It may take a few visits to the resort or a whole season. It's important not to push your children. Listen to them, and make the experience fun. Sing songs, laugh, cheer, and high-five when your child does something well. Go with friends: Your children will learn from (or teach) their friends. And don't try to focus too much on technique. Skills will come quickly, and kids learn best by watching and doing. If you do focus on technique, just pick one thing to work on.

With younger kids, start by taking them for a few runs between your legs. Hold your child tightly by the armpits and let his or her skis fall between yours. Go slow. You might be at this stage for a few hours, days, or weeks. Every child is different. Kids like the security of being between your

Skills to Work On

Here are some basic skills to work on when starting out on skis or snowboards. They will not come quickly, so be patient.

- Walking in ski or snowboard boots.
- Shuffling skis or snowboard on flat ground.
- Falling and getting up.
- Getting on and off the chairlift or rope tow.
- Snow-plowing with skis in the shape of a pizza slice, piece of pie, or Christmas tree.
- Sliding down the slope on one edge with a snowboard.
- Learning to slow and then stop.
- Turning right and left.

legs, and it may take a while for them to figure out how to stand up alone. On each run, you can slowly loosen your grip, so after several runs or visits to the resort, your child will stand up and ski without support.

While your child is between your legs, teach a snow-plow, also called a wedge. This is the basic way kids slow and stop. It is done by pointing the tips together and pressuring the inside edge of both skis. Teach kids to make a pizza slice, Christmas tree, or piece of pie. Show your child how to do it with your skis while he or she is still between your legs. This is when it's important to have a tip clip, like the Edgie-Wedgie, which holds your kid's ski tips together. It helps him or her learn how to snow-plow, and it also serves as a safety measure, to keep the skis from separating and twisting the knees.

Once your child is comfortable between your legs and you can go down the beginner slope with little help, he or she is ready to start skiing alone. There are several ways to get to the next step. Choose one method; if it doesn't work, move to another. Kids will react to these methods differently. What worked for us didn't work for our friends.

- Try a harness vest. The vest slips over a kid's ski coat and lets you hold your child by a tether attached to the vest. This keeps your child from gaining too much speed when going downhill and helps him or her stay upright. We used this for our oldest daughter, with lots of success. You can hold your child tightly between your legs at first. Then slowly let out the tether so that your child gets farther and farther out in front of you. Eventually, when your child is about ten feet in front of you, he or she will be skiing alone; the tether then serves as a backup in case one gets going too fast.
- Another method that works well is using an adult ski pole. Stand next to your child and hold an adult ski pole in your hand, parallel to the snow and in front of you. Your child holds the ski pole as well. This gives him or her something to hold onto and also allows you to control the speed. As you make more and more runs, your child will rely less and less on the pole so that eventually he or she won't need it at all.
- Another method, one that takes more parental energy, is to not use props. Slide down the hill ten feet ahead of your child, and let him or her ski into you. You act as a backstop to keep your kid from going too fast. You slide ahead, your kid skis to you. This is repeated down the slope. In general, this works best if you ski backwards or slideslip down the hill in front of your child.

As your child begins skiing solo, you need to teach him or her to slow and stop with the snow-plow. Once your little skier is skiing alone, playing

*It's never too early
to make tracks with
your kids.*

red light, green light is a fun way to help him or her master the snow-plow stop.

As they get better, teach your kids balance and fluidity by flexing knees and hips together, centering hips over feet, and keeping hands out front. The most common errors for kids are that they sit back too far and they swing their arms. So teach them to bend their knees to keep the body centered over the ski, and tell them to put their hands up as if on a steering wheel of a car.

Remember, above all, skiing should be a positive experience. Always listen to your kids, and if they want to go in for hot chocolate, don't make them take just one more run.

Snow Games

When teaching kids to ski or snowboard, try to keep it fun. If it isn't, kids might lose interest or enthusiasm. Kids love playing games on the slopes. It makes the whole experience fun, and it distracts kids from thinking too much about skiing or snowboarding skills. These games are great for all ages, especially school-age kids and early teens.

- Chase
- Follow the leader
- Treasure hunt
- Red light, green light
- Look for jumps
- Race to bottom
- Awards for the best jump, best fall, best turn
- Take pictures with a digital camera, and look at them in the lodge.

SNOWBOARD EQUIPMENT

Learning to snowboard is much harder for little kids than learning to ski. However, snowboarding is much easier for teens and adults to learn. It is difficult for young kids because you cannot just stand up, relax, and rest on a snowboard the way you can when learning to ski. You have to balance and pressure one edge or the other in snowboarding. Older kids pick it up quickly because both feet are fixed to one board, unlike skiing. If your child expresses a desire to snowboard, by all means go for it.

Boots and Bindings

Snowboard boots and bindings can be a bit confusing. There are many manufacturers, and unlike the standard bindings of skiing, snowboard boots and bindings are not standardized. The most common strap bindings work with soft boots. These boots are much like a winter pack boot, with a rubber sole and a leather or synthetic lace-up upper. The bindings have two straps that ratchet over the boot. These are less expensive than other types of snowboard boots and bindings and the most versatile. They come in small sizes for juniors and kids.

Step-in bindings, a second type, are not releasable like skis, but they allow snowboarders to quickly detach their boots from the bindings, usually by moving a quick-release lever. Hardware mounted in the sole of the boot mates with the bindings. The stiff highback part of the bindings is either attached to the binding or integrated into the boot. These are more high-performance bindings and allow kids to quickly attach and detach the board, usually without sitting in the snow like one does with strap bindings. They are not as versatile, however, because there is no industry standard. Most step-in boots work only with step-in bindings from the same company. Also, they can be a bit more expensive. I like them better because they are so easy to get in and out of. These are best for older kids who are already good snowboarders.

Okay, confused? Your best bet for younger kids if you are on a budget is to buy strap boots and bindings. The boots double as winter play boots, and they are the most versatile when you need to trade boards with a sibling or friend. For older kids who log more days on the slope, try step-in bindings such as Clickers by K2 Snowboards or one of several companies that use the Switch or Switch-compatible bindings.

Regular or goofy? Snowboarders ride with one foot forward, the same foot forward all the time. Most people are left forward, since this is usually the nondominant foot. This is called "regular foot." Few kids will ride right foot forward, but sometimes this correlates to left-hand-dominant kids. This is called "goofy foot." If they kick a soccer ball with their right foot, they are probably regular. If they are left-handed, they are likely goofy. If they ride a skateboard or scooter, they can usually tell you which foot goes forward.

Usually a shop can set up the bindings in a good learning stance. Unlike ski bindings, which are fixed in one position, snowboarders can choose the width between their feet and the degree of angle of each foot. For width, a good place to start is shoulder width. If it is too narrow or wide, it will be difficult to turn. For the angle of each foot, try 0 or 5 degrees for the back foot and 5 to 15 degrees for the front foot. Once your kid gets better at snowboarding, you can change the stance and angles. A wide and flat-angled stance is better for doing tricks or riding the half pipe. A narrow and high-angled stance is better for cruising the entire mountain.

Snowboards

Kids' snowboards, fortunately, are not too difficult to choose. The main decision is how long it should be. As with skis, the weight, age, and skill level of your child make a difference in how long the board should be. In general, shorter is better when learning. The main limitation of a board that is too short is that it doesn't float well in deep powder; usually this is not an issue for kids who are learning. Below is a rough scale for choosing a board.

- Under age five and forty pounds: 80 cm.
- Between five and seven years old and forty to sixty pounds: 90 to 100 cm.
- Between seven and nine years old and sixty to eight pounds: 110 to 120 cm.
- Between ten and twelve and eighty to one hundred pounds: 120 to 130 cm.
- Over age twelve and one hundred pounds: 130 to 150 cm.

BASIC SNOWBOARD SKILLS

Snowboarding is a lot different from skiing. You can't just shuffle or skate across the flats. You have to get your rear foot out of the binding to push yourself across the flat areas or ride the lift.

You always buckle in the forward binding first. That foot will stay strapped in when riding the snow and lifts. The rear foot needs to come out when crossing flat ground or getting on and off lifts, similar to skateboarding or riding a scooter.

Have your child practice shuffling with the front foot strapped into bindings and the rear foot out. This is how you get on and off the lift, so it's an important skill to master.

Here are some skills kids can practice on flat ground with the back foot out:

- Turn in a circle, picking up the front foot with the board attached.
- Put the rear foot on the deck and try bunny hops or shuffling.
- Skate by kicking, then gliding, as if on a skateboard or scooter.
- Learn to slow down and stop. Put the rear foot on the board, then drag the toe of the boot.
- Climb up a small incline with the board on edge.

While still on flat ground, have your child practice getting in and out of the rear foot binding. It is okay for kids to sit down to strap in, but I encourage them not to. Sitting in snow just makes them cold and wet, and it is usually not necessary. Plus, they will learn to balance quicker if they stand up while getting in and out of the rear binding.

As with skiing, it's always a good idea for kids to learn to fall and then get back up again. In general, snowboarders fall harder than skiers. It's a good idea to make that first day a sunny one, but make doubly sure the snowpack is soft. If conditions are hard and icy, it makes for big bruises. It's not a bad idea to put knee pads on kids and stuff a pair of hats in their pants to protect their bottoms.

Falling is basically a tuck and roll. Don't teach kids to break a fall by

---

Skier and Snowboarder Responsibility Code

Most ski areas have some basic safety rules. These industry-wide standards are important for kids to learn from the get-go.

- Always stay in control.
- People ahead have the right of way.
- Don't stop where you are not easily visible or where you block a slope.
- When you start downhill or merge into another slope, look uphill and yield.
- Use ski breaks or a snowboard leash to avoid a runaway ski or snowboard.
- Observe all warning signs. Stay off closed trails.
- Learn how to load, ride, and unload off a lift prior to using it.

---

putting out their hands; this is how wrist fractures occur. After a fall, kids should be able to get up on their own, although they might need help the first few days. There's no magic to it. They just bend their knees, use their hands to push off from the snow, and rock gently up to the board.

Riding the Lift

Once kids have the general idea of how to get in and out of bindings and how to slide and shuffle, they will be ready for the lift. Getting off the lift can be the most challenging aspect of the sport. Basically, without knowing how to snowboard, one is supposed to get off the chair with the back foot out of the binding and go careening down a steep ramp. Older lifts and resorts often have steep declines that were designed before snowboarding was invented. Fortunately, at newer resorts and lifts, it is easier to get off the chair without falling, especially from detachable lifts that slow down when you're getting on and off.

For your first few rides up, signal to the lift operator so he or she can slow the lift. This makes it much easier. Plan to help your child off the chair and down the hill. Kids should place the rear foot between the bindings and brace against the rear binding or the stomp pad, a padded traction plate on the board for just this purpose. They can gently slide down the ramp and drag the toe of the rear foot to slow down. If they become unstable, they can just sit down and land on their butts in the snow to stop.

Stickers make this helmet extra cool.

Going Downhill

Snowboarding is one of those sports that one learns by watching. In other words, kids should try to emulate snowboarders who can already make turns down the hill. They should start out on their heelside edge and slide sideways down the hill. Then have them sit down, turn the board around, and get up. They can then slide down on their toeside edge. This gives them an idea of the two distinct feelings of the edges.

Once they have the side slip down, both heelside and toeside, they can start going forward. It's usually easier on the heelside edge. They can traverse the slope, stop, and sit down to turn around.

After a run or two of traversing, they may be able to start turning. Beginners initiate the turn by pivoting or skidding from one edge to the other. Weight should be centered over both feet. Tell your kids to think about squeezing their knees together and turning with their feet and shins. A common mistake is that kids will just swing the back foot around. Although this might be okay for the first few runs to get the hang of turning, it is incorrect. They should press their toes and shins into a toeside turn and press their heels and calf muscles into a heelside turn. When they start turning, they should face midway between downhill and the direction of travel.

OTHER WINTER SPORTS

You can have loads of fun with your kids heading up to the mountains to play in the snow. You don't have to go to the extra expense of skiing or snowboarding. Here are some alternative activities. Much of this equipment is available for rent at winter resorts or at your local outdoor shop.

Snowshoeing

Snowshoeing is an ancient sport that has gained popularity in the last couple of years. It is loads of fun, and it's easy to do. Anyone who can walk or run can snowshoe. All you need are a pair of snowshoes, hiking or skiing poles, and warm winter clothing.

Snowshoes come in all sizes. For younger kids, small snowshoes are lighter in weight and provide plenty of flotation. Preteens and teens may be able to use adult snowshoes. Those that are around twenty-four inches in length provide plenty of flotation for most day trips for most people. Unless you are hiking in deep snow, you weigh more than two hundred pounds, or you are carrying a heavy overnight pack, you don't need anything larger.

You can find showshoe trails anywhere there are cross-country ski trails. Usually snowshoes make a separate track next to the cross-country ski track. You don't want to mess up the ski trail. Some winter resorts have designated snowshoe trails.

Mountain Safety

The mountain environment poses specific hazards, especially cold injuries like hypothermia and frostbite, and acute mountain sickness. Also, sudden storms can cause poor visibility, making it easy for one to get lost. A few simple tasks can minimize the risks of getting into trouble.
- Wear proper clothing.
- Always ski or snowboard with a buddy.
- Carry an FRS radio or cell phone.
- Carry a whistle.
- Never ski or snowboard out of bounds.
- Know how to contact the ski patrol in an emergency.
- Carry food and water.
- Consider chemical heat packs for emergencies.

Parents always get the hard part: uphill sledding.

Sledding

Sledding is fun for everyone. Many winter recreation areas have designated sledding hills. If not, check with your local ranger district to find a hill safe from avalanches or other hazards. Make sure you have a short, gentle hill and a broad, clear, flat runout. Most sledding accidents or injuries occur when kids are going too fast, have no control or way to stop, and hit a tree.

Basic cheap toboggans work pretty well for most kids. They are fast enough and durable. Some even have bars for braking. Old-fashioned sleds with runners work best for firm snow or when you are pulling your kids around the flats. They sink in deep, soft snow. I'd recommend avoiding inner tubes or plastic disks, which go too fast and are difficult to control.

Cross-Country Skiing

Some families prefer cross-country skiing over downhill skiing. Cross-country skis are readily available in kids' sizes, and there are lots of flat trails for cross-country skiers in winter recreation areas. Most winter resorts also have designated, groomed cross-country trails that are monitored by the ski patrol. Get your local shop to help size skis, boots, and poles for kids. Alternatively, go to a developed winter resort and rent for the first few days to find out if your kids like it.

10

Water Sports

My friend Paul grew up boating and fishing. When his kids were school age he decided to build a boat at a local build-your-own wooden boat factory. He spent six months building a wood dory, and his kids helped him along the way: gluing wood strips, sanding, polishing, and painting on lacquer. He took them out on the maiden voyage at our local hot spot, Lost Lake; they fished for rainbow, brook, and brown trout and brought the catch to camp for dinner. Boating not only became a regular family activity, but the whole family built the boat.

I remember many days in our trusted red canoe. Dad, my brother, and I used to take it out fishing on opening day at our local Horseshoe Lake. We reeled in trout and the occasional carp. Once, we took the canoe to Glacier National Park. We hauled it on top of our truck all the way to Montana and then down a long gravel road to the foot of Bowman Lake. Loaded with camp gear, we paddled to the head of the lake in half a day amidst huge granite peaks, clear skies, and crystal blue water. Minutes after I hooked my own trout, a bald eagle dove in and clawed a big trout of its own right next to our canoe. After a night at the head of the lake, we stashed the canoe and hiked up to the continental divide for a night. Once back to canoe camp, on day three we floated gently down the lake to our car.

Water sports are a staple pastime for outdoor kids, whether you take a dip in your local swimming hole or canoe in one of America's national parks. There are numerous water-related activities you can turn your older kids on to such as fishing, windsurfing, surfing, snorkeling, scuba diving, or a wide variety of boating, including kayaking or sailing. For example, tandem kayaks are stable and easy to paddle; they can be great for day paddling or overnight camping. Canoes are great for camping, too, because you

Reeling in a little one. Fishing is an all-time family favorite.

can cram in lots of gear (without carrying it on your back). Or choose a flat-bottom skiff, fishing boat, or sailboat.

Whatever your choice of water sports, it will be loads of fun. Your main goals should be to teach your kids to swim, educate them on safety, keep activities fun, and prevent water-related accidents and illnesses. Some experts recommend that you don't participate in boating until your kids can swim. But also remember that the cornerstone for safety is supervision. This applies to all sports but should be underscored for water-related activities. Kids should never swim or participate in water sports without parental guidance and support, even older kids. It is much more fun to play with your kids rather than sit and watch anyway. Be involved and stay available to prevent or quickly respond to accidents or mishaps.

GEARING UP

Boating can be as inexpensive or as costly as you make it. But before you buy a sailboat, canoe, or kayak, check into renting a boat or borrow one from friends. Make sure it's an activity you and your family enjoy before you make a large purchase. Fortunately, many outdoor stores, marinas, or national park concessionaires rent boats. Before you head out, here are a few items worth bringing along.

Swimsuits

Water sports clothing for kids is readily available and fortunately not too expensive. It is very size-dependent—in other words, you get less age range from certain water clothes like swimsuits and wetsuits than you do with rain or snow clothing. You can't really buy them big, and kids tend to grow out of them in one summer. Shop around, and look for deals.

You may think that any swimsuits will work, and choosing a swimsuit is simple, but it is also quite important. You should choose something that will protect your kids from sun exposure if you're in the adventure-sports mode. A T-shirt and shorts style of swimsuit works great for both boys and girls, as noted in chapter 2. It's a bonus if you can find a sun-protective long-sleeve shirt. Often called rash guards by surfers, these have become more available for kids in recent years. Since they are usually made from Lycra, they dry quickly and offer an SPF of about eight to ten. If the water is chilly, they keep kids warmer too. For bottoms, shorts are the norm for boys, but girls should wear shorts, too, instead of a swimsuit bottom. Check outdoor stores, catalogs, and internet companies.

Learning to cast: dress required, waders optional.

Gear up for sun protection on a beach trip.

Wetsuits

If you swim in cold water, you may need a wetsuit for your child. Wetsuits are readily available for kids in a number of outdoor shops or online retailers. The most versatile wetsuit is a short-sleeve short-leg wetsuit. These provide plenty of warmth for mild temperatures and some flotation too. They are also the easiest to put on. They work best for snorkeling in the tropics or sports like kayaking and rafting, where kids are not totally and constantly immersed but just getting splashed occasionally.

For cooler water, such as when surfing or snorkeling in the ocean, you may want a full-length suit, which completely covers arms and legs. In that case, kids will likely need accessories to keep them warm, which might include a neoprene hood, gloves, and booties. Wetsuits can be expensive, and your children will outgrow a wetsuit long before they will wear one out. You may not want to buy one unless you think you will use it often. Look for used wetsuits at garage sales, sports swap meets, or second-hand sports stores. Our local wetsuit shop has a trade-in policy for kids' wetsuits: Parents can trade in a used wetsuit for credit on a larger size. They keep a rack of used child-size wetsuits that are less expensive than new ones.

Footwear

You must always, always, always protect your child's feet when adventuring in and near water, even if you are just wading or tidepooling. This is a common problem among kids, who love to run barefoot on the beach, but a small cut on a foot can be debilitating for anyone, especially young kids. One step on a sharp rock, broken bottle, or seashell can ruin a whole day (or entire trip). Any old pair of canvas tennis shoes works great (leather soaks up too much water and takes too long to dry out). Kids can also wear rubber sport sandals that have straps over the instep and ankle. These are inexpensive, durable, and quick to dry. Thongs or flip-flops work okay too, but they don't stay on that well in water or when kids run.

Foul-Weather Clothing

If you are boating, make sure you have appropriate clothing for kids and adults for rain, wind, and storms. This is usually a waterproof, windproof jacket with hood, rubber boots, and warm, dry clothing underneath. Cold-weather clothing and rain gear are discussed in detail in chapter 2.

Personal Flotation Devices

Personal flotation devices, or PFDs, are essential for safety whenever you are kayaking, canoeing, rafting, or boating. Many parents use flotation aids or PFDs when swimming in lakes and streams too. Most states have laws requiring their use.

PFDs for kids are usually sized by the child's weight. Make sure it fits snug but is still comfortable. PFDs should be approved by the Coast Guard in the United States and other government agencies elsewhere. There are several types of PFDs, but the most appropriate for all-purpose use for children is Type II, as classified by the U.S. Coast Guard. Also called a near-shore buoyant vest, it is designed to float unconscious swimmers face-up in the water. For kids, it should have a groin strap to keep it from floating off a child's head and trunk and an extra flotation pad behind the head. Make sure you take your child into the store when buying one. A shop expert can help you get the correct fit. This is vitally important. See the sidebar for other types of PFDs.

Before heading out to the lake or stream, take your child to the local pool and let him or her try the PFD in the water. This lets your kid get used to swimming and jumping while wearing a PFD, and you make sure it fits well. This practice is a great exercise for safety, plus it's loads of fun and reassuring for parents.

LEARNING TO SWIM

A common question I get when I lecture about children's sports and safety is, "When should I teach my child to swim?" The answer is when you and your child are ready. That might seem like a vague answer, but the reality is you can begin laying the foundation of water skills at a very early age.

Types of PFDs

There are several types of personal flotation devices as classified by the United States Coast Guard.

- Type I is called an off-shore life jacket. These are designed to float unconscious swimmers face-up in rough water. They can be difficult to find for young kids and are bulky.
- Type II is called a near-shore buoyant vest. These are general-use life jackets that will float unconscious swimmers face-up in water. They are readily available for kids and infants. For kids, they must have a groin strap and an extra flotation pad behind the child's head and neck.
- Type III, a flotation aid, is designed to be comfortable for long periods of activity, such as when water-skiing, fishing, sailing, rafting, or kayaking. These do come in sizes for kids but will not turn an unconscious child face-up. These are better for adults or teenagers with superior swimming skills when boating in calm water and good weather.
- Type IV is a throwable device such as a life ring or a floatable seat cushion. These are usually found on boats for emergency rescue when someone who can swim needs to be rescued. They are not designed for use as a primary PFD, but rather for emergencies.
- Type V is classified as a special-use device, and examples are certain wetsuits, survival suits, or sport-specific vests for windsurfing, whitewater kayaking, or performance water-skiing. These don't have nearly as much flotation and usually are not readily available or suitable for kids.

You can start by helping your infant float in the bath tub; kids can learn to become comfortable on their backs and stomachs at a young age. Then in the pool, you can start with basic skills: back float, tummy float, basic paddling, kicking, blowing bubbles, and breath-holding. You can start this even before your child begins walking. The point is to get your young child used to water and to start the early skills of both water safety and swimming. The most common parental fears of letting kids swim at an early age are drowning and ear infections. In fact, most studies don't support the common parental concern that swimming causes ear infections. And almost all drownings of young children can be prevented with close supervision.

Don't forget to make it fun. Sing lots of songs and make games out of every swim activity. It helps to go with other kids of the same age or developmental stage as your child or even kids a bit older. It is also appropriate to keep your initial ventures into the pool short. Keep swim time to fifteen or twenty minutes with young kids.

When your children get older, you can start getting their faces wet and even dunking them. Eventually they will learn to jump in, tread water, and begin basic strokes.

My kids started at a very young age. By age one they could dunk their faces in the water. By age two they were jumping in. And at age three they were both swimming twenty feet across the pool on their own. Now my five-year-old swims the length of the pool on her front or back and participates in a swim club.

Other parents ask me how my kids learned to swim so well. I didn't do anything magical. My kids are not überathletes. Here are my secrets.

- We go swimming often—sometimes two or three times a week, especially during the rainy days of midwinter. Often we zip up to the pool for a twenty-minute dip after dinner.
- I always get in the pool with my kids. No matter what their ages, you can't teach them from poolside (and it's more difficult to supervise them).
- I make it fun—always. Play games, splash, and act goofy.
- I always pay attention to the mood and attitude of my kids. Sometimes they just want to splash and play. Other times they are motivated to work on their front crawl stroke, back float, or treading water skills.
- Inflatable rings or arm bands may help a child learn to float and swim too. Most swim teachers recommend that these flotation aids should be used sparingly, if at all. They can give some kids a false sense of security. And parents should never rely on them to support their children alone in the water. My kids used them only briefly, more as a toy than as a device to help them swim.

Remember, pay attention to warning signs of fatigue or disinterest. Take lots of breaks and listen to your children, especially if they say they are tired, hungry, or thirsty. With toddlers to preschool-age kids, you will have to carefully balance their eagerness to explore the water with safety. Set good boundaries from the beginning, such as those age-old rules posted on a rusty sign at every pool: no swimming alone, no running in the pool area, no diving or jumping where the water is shallow, and other mantras.

Lessons

Swim lessons are the foundation for the next level beyond pool play. I recommend you use a skilled instructor at your local sports club or public pool. At a young age, most children can be taught swim and survival skills as well as respect for water. Debate continues as to what age kids should start formal lessons. Early is probably okay, provided your child is ready.

My wife and I started infant lessons with our kids at about four months. The point of early lessons is to expose your child to the aquatic environment; it's more playtime than learning time. These lessons also gave us great ideas for games and early skills to work on outside of lessons.

Water survival schools for infants and toddlers are often available in large cities. Unlike standard swim lessons, these schools teach kids to float on their backs and swim to shore if they fall into a pool, hot tub, or lake. Check the internet for programs such as Swim Babes (www.swimbabes.com), Infant Swim Research (www.infantswim.com), and Baby Swimming (www.babyswimming.com). We tried it for a few months with one of my daughters, and I was amazed at how well these programs work.

For toddlers, more formal swim lessons start somewhere around one year. These are parent-child classes. The main benefits are time in the pool with your child, interaction with other parents and kids, and guidance from a swim instructor. Your child will learn basic skills like breath-holding, jumping in the pool, bubble-blowing, back-floating, and dunking his or her head underwater. These lay the foundation for basic swim strokes. As your child grows, he or she will eventually take swim lessons without you.

BOATING FOR FAMILIES

When I was a kid, we had endless days of fun in my family's bright red canoe. Now that my kids are getting older, I found myself borrowing the same canoe, now a quite faded orange, to take my own kids and grandpa paddling.

There are lots of water sports that families can enjoy. You might head to your local swimming hole with your young kids or take up surfing or whitewater rafting with your teens. Here is a short synopsis of popular water sports and tips on getting started.

Canoeing

Canoes are an all-time family favorite. They are easy to paddle and relatively inexpensive as far as boats go. The fun thing about canoes is you can

Midsummer paddling in the high lakes.

often fit the whole family in one canoe and still have room for food, fishing gear, and warm clothes. And it usually fits on top of a family minivan or SUV without too much trouble. Usually canoes have two or three seats for paddlers. But you may prefer to have your children sit on a pad on the bottom of the canoe. This way, your kids will be lower in the boat and less likely to fall out. If you want to go canoe camping, you can take plenty of gear without having to haul it in a backpack.

You do have to supervise kids, and since canoes can be tipped over, it's better not to bring young kids in canoes until they can swim. Also, leave your dog at home. It may sound like fun, but you'll have your hands full enough with your kids. Dogs can't easily grasp the concept of floating in a boat on the water.

Don't forget: Let your older kids help with, or do most of, the paddling.

Kayaking

Kayaking is a great sport that older kids will love. You will probably start with sea kayaks, also called touring kayaks. Sea kayaks are wide and long; they have a rudder to improve tracking and stability. Unlike their whitewater cousin, sea kayaks are quite easy to paddle and very difficult to capsize. They have a hatch or two to store lunch and dry clothes.

Dad needs a rest when tandem kayaking.

Some families with young kids might prefer tandem sea kayaks so they can paddle with their kids and keep a close eye on them. Older kids, especially teens, may want their own boat. Stay together at all times.

If you don't have your own, many lake or beach resorts rent sea kayaks. It can get a bit expensive to outfit a family of four in kayaks, so renting is a great way to try the sport without spending lots of money. If you rent, make sure the weather is nice, and be on guard for currents, waves, eddies, and swift water. If you buy, you may have to get a special roof rack to haul them on your car.

Whitewater Rafting

Whitewater rafting can be an adventure of a lifetime, especially if you set your sights on the Grand Canyon. It is a sport common to almost every state. In fact, you don't even need your own gear: You'll find a multitude of outfitters that rent gear and provide guides for many rivers. You'll have some excitement blasting through rapids, as well as quiet time drifting down tranquil stretches. This is a great way to interact with your kids and blend adventure with family time. Gentle rafting is great for blended, extended, or large families. It's loads of fun for all ages, especially if you have a wide age range between kids or grandma and grandpa want to come along.

If you want to plan a river trip, look for outfitters close to your home. Try to find a half-day trip for your first river. Usually this includes about two to three hours on a river with some basic instruction and equipment preparation before the float. For the more adventurous, you can find raft trips that vary from one day to two weeks. Unless you are skilled and have experience and rafting equipment, it's best to join a guided trip with an outfitter.

Rivers are classified by how big their rapids are. Class 0 means no rapids, just a tranquil float along with the current. Class 1 has gentle ripples. Class 2 has larger rapids that a raft can easily cruise through but a kayaker may find a bit of a challenge. Classes 3, 4, and 5 are bigger rapids, waterfalls, and technical sections of a river best left to experts.

Save whitewater rafting until your kids are older, say, at least ten or twelve. This sport can be physically demanding. Your child should be a strong swimmer, in case he or she gets tossed out of the boat in rapids or swift water.

Boating

Boating is another fun water sport for all ages and ranges from rowboats and dinghies to large sailboats and rental motor yachts. You might want to take your kids fishing on a lake or in the ocean or tour a group of islands in a sailing vessel. Small boats can be towed behind your car on a trailer. You can rent larger boats at a marina.

Open-water boating requires special skill and equipment. Help may not be readily available on the water. Storms may come up suddenly, and currents and tides can be dangerous. You'll need a survival and first aid kit consistent with open-water boating and the knowledge and skill to navigate in marine waterways.

Surfing

Surfing is a great outdoor sport that is actually quite old—the natives of Polynesia surfed ocean waves. Waves can be surfed on almost any coastline in the world, and a surfboard and a wetsuit for each person are all you need. This is a physically demanding sport for kids and parents. It takes some time to teach your kids surfing, so be patient.

Most parents start with a long board, hold it steady, and allow their kids to ride the small breaking whitewater near shore. Choose a gentle beach with tiny waves. The water should be shallow enough for parents to stand up in it. Some parents prefer to ride tandem, in other words, on the same board with their kids. Others may choose to get their kids up on the

Skim boarding in the shore break, this child enjoys the waves the easy way.

Body boarding is a great way to enjoy the surf.

board and then let go. Whatever the case, be patient, take your time, and take lots of breaks.

There are many variations of surfing. Body surfing is when one floats on waves without a board. Body boarding is a sport similar to surfing in which one lies prone on a short foam board. Skim boarding is when one hydroplanes across the water at the edge of the surf. All three are much easier than surfing. Above all, be careful of ocean waves, currents, and undersea creatures.

Snorkeling

Snorkeling is great for families. It's inexpensive, you can snorkel on almost any beach or while on a tropical vacation, and you can all go together, yet still have some independence. You will simply need swim fins, masks, and snorkels for everyone. Try to get a quality mask that fits your child. Rent if you are taking a trip to the tropics or to a beach resort and you don't want to bring a set.

As with any water sport, beware of currents, spiny creatures, and sun. Wear shoes if you don't have fins. Wear a sun-protective shirt (not a skimpy

The well-outfitted snorkeler is safe and warm.

Water Safety

Remember, different sports and different types of water pose special hazards.

If you are at sea or in open water, be aware of waves, currents, swells, and storms. Near surf beaches, you may have breaking waves, rip currents, littoral currents, undertows, and logs or other debris in the surf. Be extra cautious, and if you are in open ocean conditions, you need special skills for communicating from ship to shore. Be prepared with clothing, life preservers, and emergency kits, which are beyond the scope of this book.

For inland streams and lakes, watch for submerged logs and rocks, rapids, currents, eddies, waterfalls, and other hazards. Kayakers, canoeists, and rafters should be skilled in swift-water rescue. This is a specialized technique that requires professional instruction, especially when trying to free a boat or rescue a person from rapids. Fortunately, there are many courses available on swift-water safety and rescue. Check your local outfitter or raft shop or the internet.

Most accident prevention is common sense. Here's a checklist for parents.
- Teach your children to swim.
- Always get in the water with your kids.
- Take lots of breaks.
- Be careful of sun exposure.
- Watch for cold water temperatures.
- Guard against polluted water.
- Use shoes to protect feet from rocks, sticks, or shells that can cause injury.
- For sports like kayaking, rafting, and surfing, wear an ASTM-approved water-sports helmet.
- Clean all cuts and scrapes promptly with clean water and apply a water-resistant bandage.
- Keep snacks, drinking water, and dry clothes handy.
- Use an approved PFD.

swimsuit). If you don't have a sun shirt, a white cotton T-shirt or a synthetic long-underwear top works just fine.

If you go with school-age kids, hold hands. This is a great way to make sure you stick together while looking at the sea.

11

Rock Climbing

My kids, like all kids, love climbing: rocks, trees, or the fort in our yard play set. To satisfy their urge and introduce them to a sport I love, I built a six-foot-high climbing wall and attached it to my kids' play set. First I cut and bolted a piece of heavy-duty plywood to the side near the ladder. Then my kids helped me paint it bright purple (they picked out the paint on a trip to the hardware store). Then we attached climbing holds, which are made from a lightweight cementlike composite material. Climbers grab holds with their hands and step on them with their feet to ascend or descend. We got two dozen holds about the size of half an apple from a local manufacturer. They came in bright colors and were inexpensive. Now my kids have a six-foot-high climbing wall they can ascend or descend, with me spotting them of course. At the top of the wall we have a bike bell my kids can honk. Only once, please!

For young kids, climbing is just a part of growing up. Older kids love to climb large boulders, big trees, or even a climbing wall at school. Rock climbing is a great sport to improve your child's agility, balance, hand-eye coordination, and finesse. If you don't climb, this is a fantastic opportunity to learn a sport with your kids, especially teenagers. You will start out on even footing, but be advised: Your child may quickly become a better climber than you. Lack of fear, light weight, and agile motion allow kids to advance rapidly. Nonetheless, rock climbing is one of those sports that all skill levels can participate in together.

Your kids can learn to climb at a young age. Some people feel kids should be at least preteenage before they start rock climbing. That's probably a good idea. For climbing, proper equipment and professional instruction are vitally important. With younger children, you don't want them to misunderstand the concept of a rope used for safety. You don't want your

Plan a climb when your kids are older.

child climbing a boulder or tree too big for their skill. If you have any doubt, wait until your kids are in middle school.

Above all, this sport requires formal instruction from a climbing instructor at a gym or school. The instructor should not be just a parent or teacher; he or she should be specially trained to teach climbing. Check out an indoor climbing wall or climbing gym. I live in a small town, but we still have two climbing walls. Our local sports club has a climbing wall where members or nonmembers can take lessons, and our junior high school has a climbing wall as well. Kids can take climbing lessons while in school or during summer break with community education classes. In fact, during the summer county fair, a portable climbing wall comes on a truck for kids to practice on.

AN INTRODUCTION
There are several types of climbing; bouldering, top roping, and free climbing are the most basic. This chapter provides just a basic introduction.

Bouldering
When your kids climb walls close to the ground, they generally don't need a rope, as long as you spot them. This means they are always within a few

feet of the ground, so a fall is only a short distance. Often they just put their foot on the ground or jump a couple feet. If they do fall, you can spot or catch them. Like a gymnast falling off a low balance beam, sometimes kids just need a hand or help jumping to the ground. Climbers call this bouldering because it's often done on large boulders sitting on the ground.

Top Roping

A second style of climbing is called top roping. Anytime a fall could be more than a couple feet, you will need a rope. The climber is tied on at one end. The rope goes up to the top of the climbing wall and through two large bolts, called anchors. Then a parent or instructor holds the other end and keeps a climber from going more than a foot or two when he or she falls. When kids are learning, the instructor will keep a tight rope with little or no slack. Thus when the climber lets go of the wall or loses footing, he or she doesn't fall but leans against the rope for support. In fact, an attentive belayer can keep the rope very tight so that when a climber loses grip or footing, there is no fall at all. The climber just hangs on the rope.

A climbing instructor or expert parent prevents a climber from falling by using a belay. A belay is a method for pulling in the slack rope as the climber ascends, but allowing for a quick lock if the climber falls, called braking. For example, as a child climbs up, the excess rope is pulled in using the belay. If the child falls, the belayer quickly locks the rope. This is a skill that requires professional instruction, lots of practice, and experience.

Free Climbing

Free climbing is an advanced method that is beyond the basic introduction provided here. Free climbing means a climber doesn't use the protective rope that is anchored to the top of a climbing wall. Instead, the climber attaches the rope to anchors while he or she climbs. These are either prefixed bolts or temporary anchors that the climber places while he or she ascends.

GEARING UP

You'll probably use the equipment provided at your local climbing gym when starting out. This brief overview provides only general information about basic equipment. You should rent the equipment from a climbing gym or seek out a climbing shop with a skilled employee who can help you assemble the proper equipment.

Lightweight loose-fitting clothing works best for indoor climbing. Try long sweat pants for kids. Shorts tend to ride up, and the harness can become uncomfortable against the legs.

When bouldering kid style, make sure you spot your children.

If your kids are starting out, rubber-soled sneakers work okay for the first day. After they get the hang of climbing, they might want to try specially designed climbing shoes, usually available to rent at climbing gyms. These tight-fitting shoes look like slippers or elf shoes. They have a specially designed sole made from rubber that has superior grip on the climbing-wall holds. Pointy narrow shoes provide better purchase on small climbing holds.

A chalk bag is a small nylon pouch filled with powdered gymnastic chalk. Just as in gymnastics, this is used to minimize sweat and oil from a climber's hands to provide a better grip. Usually the bag is clipped to the belt or pants of the climber's back so it is out of the way but accessible to both hands.

If one is bouldering, clothing, shoes, and a chalk bag will suffice. But to top rope, a climber needs a harness. A harness is a sling made from webbing that fits around your child. For young kids, a seat-chest combination is the best. This keeps them upright if they fall. You don't want them to fall, then flip upside down and bang their heads against the climbing wall. For teenagers, a waist harness may be sufficient, since they can usually keep themselves upright when they fall while using a top rope. You will want an expert at a shop or your climbing instructor to fit the harness. It should be snug with no loose straps. The rope is then tied into the harness.

The instructor will also have a harness. But instead of tying the rope directly into the harness like the climber, the instructor will use a belay system. The belay system usually uses a belay device, which is an aluminum tube or figure-eight-shaped device. These let the rope pass through freely when a climber is ascending. With a fall, the rope can be quickly locked to prevent a serious long fall. The belay device is clipped to the instructor's harness using a large spring clip known as a carabiner.

A belay device and carabiner are important for the belayer, usually an instructor or a parent who is an expert rock climber. It's best to use the belay device and carabiner at the school or climbing gym. If you buy your own, discuss the different types and styles with the shop expert.

Ropes are actually a complex piece of equipment designed specifically for a certain type of climbing. Not only do you need to choose the correct rope for the style of climbing, you need to care for it properly, inspect it routinely, and replace it regularly. This takes formal instruction beyond the scope of this book. Indoor rock gyms and schools usually provide ropes.

Technical climbing equipment like a harness, belay device, carabiner, rope, shoes, and other gear needs to be chosen carefully. Different styles and varieties are used for different types of climbing. Also, the gear should be cared for properly: stored, cleaned, inspected, and retired when appropriate.

STARTING OUT

Generally, kids will start out bouldering; in other words, they will stay low to the ground as described above. Teach them to always keep three or four extremities on the climbing wall—move only one foot or hand at a time. Also, teach kids to climb both up and down; it can be more difficult to descend. They should learn that whatever they climb up, they should be able to climb down.

Always spot your kid closely to catch or support him during a fall. As your child gains skills, he shouldn't necessarily rely on you. He should climb within his limits to avoid falling. If he wants to push his skills a bit, make sure he is close to the ground. That way, if he tries a difficult move and falls, he can put his foot down on the ground or jump a few feet. It's best if he can land on wood chips, pea gravel, or some other forgiving surface. Climbing gyms sometimes have big pads or soft shredded rubber to land on.

For top roping, an instructor will help you get set with your kids. You have to put the harness on correctly and tie the rope on using a double figure-eight knot. Make sure the rope goes through the anchors at the top of the wall and your belayer is ready. Climbers use age-old jargon to communicate. Your child should first check to see if the instructor has locked him into the belay; then he needs to notify his instructor that he is ready to climb. It goes like this:

Student climber: "Belay on?" to ask if the belayer is ready.

Instructor belayer: "On belay." This means the instructor has the student locked into the belay.

Student climber: "Climbing." This signals that the climber is ready to start.

Instructor belayer: "Climb on." This gives the go-ahead for the climber to start climbing.

This double-speak might seem redundant, but it was designed specifically to check and then double-check the system. It lets the climber know that he is locked into the safety system, and that the belayer is ready for him to start climbing.

CLIMBING SAFETY

Climbing is a complex, advanced sport, but if your teen shows interest, consider learning together. Safety is of vital importance with this sport, especially considering all the technical equipment required and the risk of falling. There are a number of general safety issues you should keep in mind.

- Always spot your children if they are bouldering.
- If climbing, kids and parents should be supervised by an instructor.
- Make sure your child's harness fits correctly, the knot is tied properly, and the belay system is set up correctly.
- Ropes, harnesses, belay devices, and carabiners can all fail. You should take lessons from a climbing gym or school and use their equipment.
- All equipment needs to be cared for and stored and cleaned properly. It should be inspected regularly and retired at the appropriate time.
- Wear a helmet designed and approved for climbing.
- Don't teach your child to be fearful of climbing; teach him or her to be cautious, smart, and attentive to detail.
- If you or your child has any question about the skills of the belay person (especially if it is a novice parent or another child), don't climb with that person. Wait for the instructor at the climbing gym or school.

Part 3

ADVENTURE AFOOT:
Fifty Excellent Family Adventures

We have a poster-size calendar in our house that we use as the master schedule. Mom and Dad's work schedules are in red, kids' activities in pencil, and family trips or vacations in blue. This is our life in a snapshot. Seems compulsive, but it has become an effective and essential method for keeping track of my family's busy lives, especially protecting valuable time for trips, vacations, and adventures. Sometimes the only way we can assure that we can get away to the coast for a few days is to block off a weekend on the calendar months in advance.

In addition to a master calendar, every outdoor family should have some sort of wish list. My list of activities, places, and adventures is long and runs many years in advance. I have cool day trips, local overnights, and trips of a lifetime on mine. Many we've already completed, some are in planning mode for later this year, and others are planned way out in advance.

After consulting my list, as well as lists and ideas from my friends and colleagues who are outdoor adventure parents, I've collected the fifty most excellent trips for outdoor families. There is something for everyone here, ranging from basic day trips to elaborate once-in-a-lifetime adventures. It is designed to appeal to a broad range of budgets, ages, and interests. You can plan to do one or more of these trips or use the ideas to create your own. If you have fun, plan to do the same trip again. It's exciting to explore new places, but it's also fun to return to a familiar place time and again.

Hang on and get ready to blast off. And one word of advice: Once you mention a special trip to your children, they may not forget it.

12

Ten Local Activities for All Ages and Budgets

When you start out adventuring, you're probably looking for simple, low-budget adventures. Depending on your children's ages, you'll choose different activities and different levels of intensity. Here are some time-tested trips for all ages and all budgets. They work great for extended, blended, and large families, and they are rewarding for solo time: one parent, one child.

Remember, try to keep things simple and don't try to do too much. A half-day activity is just perfect for most days when you're staying close to home. That way, you won't be overwhelmed with packing and planning. Pack a good lunch, bring extra water and snacks, throw in rain boots and jackets, and off you go.

1. HIKE

You can hike almost anywhere in almost any weather. Many communities have paved walking paths or hiking trails; these are great for little kids and grandma and grandpa. Or look for a nearby city, county, or state park with a nature trail. Hiking is a basic activity you can enjoy with no extra burden on your pocketbook. Don't try to get fancy, and don't try to go too far. If you have school-age or adolescent children, you might have to run to keep up. Don't forget to stop and enjoy nature: Look at flowers, cool bugs, or clouds. Find a smooth flat rock in the sun for lunch or dip your feet in a bubbling brook.

On one hike, we found a goose egg atop a clump of grass at our local park. "Don't touch it, it will hatch someday," I explained. Another time a broken beer bottle forced me into a long oration about garbage: "Why is it there, Papa?" Sometimes we collect neat sticks or colored stones. Pay atten-

Group photo at sundown, smiles all around.

tion to your children's interests and activity level. Sometimes they might be in the mood to hike fast, get up a good sweat, and not really talk much. Other times it might be a good opportunity for you to discuss important school issues with your teenager.

2. THROW ROCKS

Like any child, my kids love throwing rocks. The problem is, they can't throw stones just anywhere or anytime, so to satisfy their urge, we often go down to the river and do nothing but throw rocks. This is both great fun and a good lesson. They get to practice their throwing skills and at the same time satisfy their desire to huck stones. Also, it's fun to watch them splash, and sometimes we play games. We try to outdistance each other's throw or try to hit wave rings created by each other's splashes. There's another lesson too: I am very careful to always reinforce that the only place they can throw rocks is in the river with mom or dad present, supervising them closely. Under no circumstance can they throw rocks elsewhere. Because we do this often, my kids know that's a strict rule.

3. BIKE

No matter the age, your kids will love to pedal. It's a great skill that every child will need to learn sooner or later. Plus it's a fun family activity, especially for mixed families or those with a wide gap between kids' ages.

Depending on your children and their ages, you might be teaching them to ride a bike for the first time, you might be working off those training wheels, or you might be exploring a new dirt trail.

For younger kids, make an adventure out of riding bikes. We often pack up and drive down to our local park. It has a huge parking lot that is generally empty most sunny days in winter. The vast expanse of asphalt is smooth and gated. In fact, this is such a popular activity in my town that we often run into friends. The kids will ride circles, chase sea gulls, and laugh. Sometimes we take our bikes down to the local skateboard park (before school gets out), or we hit the five-mile paved bike path. This trail is off limits to cars, so it is safer than roads. It travels through thick woods, and we often spy deer, squirrels, or chipmunks. There is an ice cream store at the end too.

If you can, look for an abandoned dirt or gravel road for a taste of mountain biking. Our town's single track is perfect for preteens or teenagers because it parallels a gravel road. Anytime kids get tired of riding, they can hop off the dirt trail and cruise back to the car on the road. Although it is mostly flat, it has a few challenging hills and a couple stream crossings that yield laughs as big as the splashes.

4. PLAY IN THE SNOW

If you can't afford the time and expense of skiing, head to your local mountain recreation area and play in the snow. There is plenty of fun to be had building snow forts, making snow angels, or romping in the white wonderland.

Try snowshoeing. Anyone who can walk and run can snowshoe—it is that easy. You can find many outdoor stores that rent snowshoes. If you buy, they are much less expensive than skis. And they come in kids' sizes too. It's a great activity for the whole family, especially if you want to bring grandma and grandpa along, provided they are in good shape.

Sledding is another all-time family winter favorite that you can do almost anywhere you can find snow. You probably have a favorite sledding hill at your park or in your backyard. If you live near mountains, sledding is an easy half-day junket. Pack up the car with winter clothes, lunch, and a thermos of hot chocolate.

Most winter recreation areas have designated trails or hills that are safe for snowshoeing and sledding. Check with your local sports shop or ranger station. Some ski resorts have sledding hills and snowshoeing trails too.

5. GO BOATING

Kids love water and boating. Take older kids who are strong swimmers out for a paddle on the lake. Rent a boat or borrow one from friends. Try a basic rowboat or a canoe for starters. Make sure everyone has a life vest and knows how to swim. Don't try to go too far your first day, and don't go out if the water or weather conditions are poor. You'll have loads of fun paddling or rowing around checking out inlets and swamps. For a more advanced trip with older kids, rent a tandem sea kayak. Bring a fishing pole, binoculars for birding, or a book for when you tie up under a tree or stop at a sandy beach.

6. TAKE A ROAD TRIP
Get in the car and travel to any cool outdoor spot at the spur of the moment. It might be a local park, nature preserve, or play park. It might be a favorite waterfall. Get out, keep it simple, and have fun. It doesn't have to be complicated. Sometimes we drive up to the high school and visit the animals in the 4-H barn. We've been known to put on old clothes and splash in mud puddles in our neighborhood. On another great trip, we ride bikes down to our favorite summer hangout: Mike's Ice Cream. Sometimes we take a road trip to the city: We can visit the zoo, forestry center, children's museum, or science center.

7. SWIM
If you're looking for an inexpensive family activity in the hot days of mid-summer, head to your local watering hole, river, or beach to splash and wade in the water. Hopefully, you have a lake or swimming hole in your community. It's best if it's a public beach or park with a lifeguard. If not, make sure you swim with your kids and avoid swift water. Don't forget sunscreen, sun hats, and sunglasses.

8. PACK AN ADVENTURE LUNCH
You've heard of the power lunch; you've heard of the picnic. Now, take your kids on an adventure lunch. Anywhere you can find some trees, cool shade, a large meadow, or a small creek is a good spot for an adventure lunch. Pack a lunch, and don't forget to bring some special treats. Once there, your kids will want to explore, run, and play. Throw rocks in the water, build sand castles, or play chase. You may want to bring a Frisbee or a soccer ball. Count the flowers and ants. Or watch birds and clouds. When it's time for lunch, spread out the picnic, and let your kids serve you. They will have a ball.

9. GO FISHING
There's something special about children catching their first fish. Their eyes will light up and they will be stoked with excitement. You will probably need to discuss the circle of life and the food chain with younger kids. They

Supervise your kids, yet let them learn their limits.

will have questions, and this is a great time to educate them. You may choose the style of fishing that is catch-and-release, which means you let the fish go without killing them. Alternatively, you might be catching fish for food, in which case you can clean the fish and then cook it for dinner.

You don't have to spend big bucks for a fishing pole. A rod and reel plus a few hooks and bait can be inexpensive. Go shopping for tackle with your kids or surprise them with a birthday present of a new rod and reel. They can help dig nightcrawlers for bait the night before you head out too. Bring and teach lots of patience, if the fish are not biting.

Helpful hints: Teach kids to cast in the backyard without a hook. Make sure you have the appropriate fishing licenses. Know the catch laws, including size requirements and limits.

10. PARTICIPATE IN COMMUNITY EDUCATION

Many schools and community education programs have outdoor classes that can introduce you and your kids to a number of new sports or outdoor activities. And if you enroll your child in a class, you can often rent the equipment so you can see if he or she likes the sport first. It's double fun if you can learn a sport with your child, especially if it is one that he or she picked out. Or, find an activity that he or she can do with friends. Usually these classes are taught by local experts, who can be a great resource for getting inexpensive equipment or finding good local spots to participate in the activity.

13

Ten of the Best National Parks for Families

A visit to a national park is a fantastic family experience. You may have one in your own state, or you might choose to travel to one of the premier national parks in the U.S. All have something for a wide variety of ages and abilities. You can hike, bike, and camp in most. Choose boating, fishing, surfing, scuba diving, tidepooling, wading, snorkeling, or rowing in those with water. Try something simple like stargazing, bird watching, or plant identification.

Most parks have family-friendly trails, extensive visitors centers, and excellent camping that ranges from primitive backcountry tent spots to full-hookup RV sites. If you have little kids or you are not quite ready for camping, choose from many lodging options like a park-operated lodge or cabin or a private inn in a nearby town.

Almost all national parks have a Junior Ranger program. These programs involve the gamut of ages—from preschoolers to teens—in a variety of activities. Many have interactive websites that kids can view before your trip. Once at a park, pick up an age-specific activity booklet at the visitors center that includes coloring, games, guides, and stories. Many visitors centers have movies or exhibits geared specifically for kids. They introduce the natural and cultural history of the park and get kids excited about outdoor adventure. Ranger-led programs are a great way to explore the parks. They may include short hikes, campfire tales, beach walks, stargazing sessions, or a group bike ride. For older kids, wildlife and plant programs, nature discussions, naturalist-in-residence walks, scientific studies, and social science programs can be great fun and educational. With little ones, check out the self-guided interpretive trails.

Here is a small sample of the best and most famous national parks for families. They are scattered through a wide geographic area and provide a

Don't try to overdo it; take a break on the hike.

broad range of family activities. See the next chapter for water-based or beach-oriented national parks and national seashores.

For more information, you can check one central website, www.nps.gov. This has links to every national park, seashore, lakeshore, and monument. You'll find everything from kids' activities to camping reservations on the individual park websites.

1. ARCHES
The muted red sandstone of the southern Utah desert, called slickrock, is a beautiful scenic treat and a fabulous playground for all ages. The labyrinth canyonlands are like no other place for hiking. Kids and adults alike will have a ball among the mazes, box canyons, and mesas. Southern Utah has numerous parks, including Zion, Cedar Breaks, Capitol Reef, Bryce, and Canyonlands. Arches is one of the most accessible. You can hike to the famed Delicate Arch and learn about the fascinating geologic history of the fins, pinnacles, balanced rocks, macrobiotic soil, and amazing colors, contrasts, and textures. The scenic desert is contrasted with the snowcapped La Salle Mountains, providing an amazing mix of desert and high country.

Access to Arches is usually via Salt Lake City, Utah, or Grand Junction, Colorado. You will then need a car to make the four- or two-hour trip, respectively. Arches is super hot in summer, with temperatures upwards of

100 degrees in July. Thunderstorms can pop up out of the clear blue sky in midsummer. A small spat of rain can cause a flash flood in a narrow, deep canyon, so it's best to visit during spring or fall. Camping is available in Devils Garden. For lodging, try nearby Moab.

2. DENALI

Alaska is a true wilderness adventure that is best perhaps for older kids. Denali is home to 20,320-foot Mount McKinley, the tallest peak in North America, as well as huge glacial valleys in the Alaska Range. The six-million-acre subarctic ecosystem is replete with grizzly bears, wolves, Dall sheep, and moose. The park is accessible by car via Denali Park Road for fifteen miles to Savage River Bridge. Beyond that you will need to ride a shuttle or tour bus.

It is easiest to fly into Anchorage and take a rental car, shuttle, commuter flight, or train to the park, 240 miles away. The bustling outdoor town of Talkeetna, 140 miles south of the park, is mountaineering HQ. It's said there are four seasons in Alaska: June, July, August, and Winter. With kids, visit Denali in summer. Whereas most of the year can be cool, damp, rainy, and dark, summers can be mild and sunny, with highs up to the mid-60s. Nonetheless, you'll still want warm coats, hats, and boots for everyone. Riley Creek campground is near the entrance and open all year. RV sites are available, since that's a very popular way to tour Alaska.

3. GLACIER

High alpine meadows, cold clear lakes, huge granite peaks, and thick forests make Glacier a favorite for families. Large predators, hundreds of bird species, and over seven hundred miles of trail supplement the geologic beauty. You may not see the elusive grizzly bear, so look also for bighorn sheep, mountain goats, coyotes, and wolves. Along with Canada's Waterton Lakes National Park, Glacier makes up Waterton-Glacier International Peace Park. For a more adventurous trip, plan a canoe camping trip on one of the many lakes or hike to the Continental Divide. Keep your eyes peeled for bald eagles.

Fly into beautiful Flathead Valley via Glacier Park International Airport in Kalispell, Montana. Glacier is an hour's drive. West Glacier is the hub of summer activity, and you'll probably start by driving the Going-to-the-Sun Road. Glacier's northern climate can be rainy and cool or warm and sunny. Even in summer, high elevations and nights can be cool. Snow can occur anytime too: a foot in August one year. The park has thirteen campgrounds with one hundred sites, including backcountry, car camping, and RV spots. There is lodging in West Galcier, or check out Glacier's historic backcountry lodges, built at the turn of the century. Check in the Apgar Visitors Center to get the scoop on bear sightings and precautions.

4. GRAND CANYON

Grand Canyon National Park is one of our most unique and wondrous parks. It begins at Lees Ferry below Glen Canyon Dam and ends at Grand Wash Cliffs, before the huge Lake Mead. Roughly two thousand million years old, the canyon is almost one mile deep from rim to river and ten miles wide. For the most family-friendly activities and amenities, start at the South Rim. Check out the Canyon View Information Center and the museums that highlight Pueblo Indian life from eight hundred years ago and the canyon's rich geologic history. To avoid crowds, plan a trip from the North Rim, open seasonally.

You can fly into Las Vegas, Phoenix, Flagstaff, and Grand Canyon Airport in Yusayan, just near South Rim. Rent a car or take a shuttle to the South Rim. Although this is desert, the rim is seven thousand feet above sea level. Hot days and cool nights are the norm spring through fall. However, once you hike down into the canyon, it's like a pressure cooker. Temperatures get up to 120 in midsummer. Take lots of water and be careful of sunburn and heat stroke. There are numerous camping and lodging opportunities at the South Rim. Adventurous travelers who don't want to tent camp should consider Phantom Ranch, a backcountry dormitory and cabin at river level on the floor of the canyon.

5. GREAT SMOKY MOUNTAINS

Located in Tennessee and North Carolina, Great Smoky Mountains National Park includes diverse forests, ancient mountains, and Southern Appalachian culture and is easily accessible by eastern seaboard adventurers. In fact, this is the largest protected area in the East. Check out water-powered grist mills or the environmental education program that integrates natural and cultural history. The park's interactive website has links to Appalachian Highlands Science Learning Center, Great Smoky Mountains Institute at Tremont, and Smokey Mountain Field School. These offer a variety of workshops, hikes, family adventures, and plant, wildlife, and history programs.

Fly into McGhee-Tyson Airport in Alcoa, Tennessee, about forty-five miles from the park, or Asheville Airport in North Carolina, about sixty miles east. The broad range of elevation, from 800 to over 6,500 feet, gives the Great Smoky Mountains a wide climate range. The park is often mild year-round, with cool weather on the hilltops and warmer temperatures in valleys. Summer is hot and humid. Fall has warm days, cool nights, and less humidity. Multiple campgrounds are located in this park, from full RV hookups to year-round backcountry spots. Check out horse camps or LeConte Lodge, atop 6,593-foot Mount LeConte (you've got to hike up).

6. MOUNT RAINIER

Mount Rainier is a humongous active volcano. This gigantic glacier-clad peak is supported by thick old-growth forest, subalpine meadows, and spectacular summer wildflowers. Look for white-tailed or black-tailed deer, coyotes, red foxes, Douglas squirrels, elk, golden-mantled ground squirrels, and birds. Some trails are so popular, like the Wonderland that circumnavigates the mountain, that they are booked nearly a year in advance. Check out the large Jackson Visitors Center at Paradise, which has exhibits on natural and cultural history, including mountain climbing history. The Longmire Museum has natural and cultural history and a transportation exhibit.

You can reach the park via airports in Seattle, Washington, or Portland, Oregon. The most common access is via the Nisqually entrance near Ashford, Washington. Narrow roads and large crowds can make it difficult to find parking or camping. Summers can have spectacular days of sun as well as the Pacific Northwest's famed liquid sunshine. Bring a raincoat and boots for any time of year. The best weather is midsummer through early fall. In winter, deep snow is the norm. The park once held the most-snow-per-winter record, with 1,122 inches of snow in 1971–72 season. There are many campgrounds, but they tend to fill up in summer. Paradise Inn, the famous staging area for summit climbs, has rooms to rent.

7. OLYMPIC

This fascinating temperate rainforest is sandwiched between huge glaciated peaks and the rugged Pacific Coast. The biological diversity of the three ecosystems includes eight plants and fifteen animals that are not found anywhere else on earth. The lush Hoh Rainforest is wet—you should be prepared for the twelve feet of rain per annum. Check out Hurricane Ridge area for a taste of high alpine mountains or the wild and rugged Rialto or Ruby beaches on the coast.

By air, fly into Seatac Airport near Seattle. You can drive three hours to the park or take a commuter flight to Port Angeles. The Washington State historic ferry system provides car access; this can be a special treat for kids. The weather year-round is, well, wet. The best chance for dry weather is from midsummer to early fall, but crowds will be large. The many campgrounds can fill up in summer. There are some lodges and cabins in the park too.

8. ROCKY MOUNTAIN

Massive mountain peaks along the Continental Divide, most more than 13,000 feet high, provide the backdrop for this less-crowded park. Elk, mule deer, bighorn sheep, moose, coyotes, and a great many small critters scamper through large meadows of endless wildflowers. Try to visit during the fall elk-mating season, called the rut. Or hike up to the Continental Divide and back. Check out Moraine Park Museum, which highlights the park's natural history and begins with a half-mile interpretive nature trail. Or try the Never Summer Ranch, maintained as a 1920s dude ranch.

Fly into Denver International Airport and drive up to the park. Like in many mountain parks, the temperature can be cool, even in summer. In fall or spring you can get snow. Midsummer has many typical Colorado days: sun, clear sky, and more sun. Numerous campgrounds give lots of options for overnighters.

9. YELLOWSTONE

Yellowstone National Park is America's oldest and one of the most popular for families. It was founded in 1872 and has over 10,000 hot springs and geysers. The geothermal wonders span half the park. Old Faithful Geyser is the most famous, but you'll find many sizes and colors of boiling calderas and geysers all over this park. Among other wildlife, grizzly bears, bison, elk, and now wolves range free. Don't miss the Museum of the National Park Ranger, which shows the history of the park ranger profession. Older kids will like Expedition: Yellowstone, a week-long program located in Lamar Buffalo Ranch that teaches natural history, cultural history, and ecology through hikes, dramatics, writing, and discussions.

The main gateway is West Yellowstone, Montana. By air, you can fly to Jackson, Wyoming, or Bozeman, Montana, if you want to drive in from the north. A seasonal airport operates in West Yellowstone. Summertime temperatures range in the 70s, with cool nights. Thunderstorms are common during summer afternoons. Winter blankets the park with snow, so access is by snowmobile or snowcat. There are many campgrounds, including those suitable for RVs. Park-run lodges and cabins as well as private hotels are available. Consider the Old Faithful Inn, Lodge Cabins, or Snow Lodge near the Old Faithful Geyser.

10. YOSEMITE

Yosemite's spectacular Sierra Nevada Mountains are not to be missed: huge granite domes, sharp peaks, luscious valleys, giant sequoias, tall waterfalls, and expansive meadows chock full of wildflowers. Plus, this is rock climbing central. Hike in the Mariposa Grove of giant sequoias, check out the wildflowers of Tuolumne meadows, or head to Glacier Point for the breathtaking view. Don't miss Yosemite Museum, which has displays of Miwok and Paiute tribes, including basket-weaving, beadwork, and games. The Ahwahnee village is reconstructed with American Indian cultural demonstrations.

Many flights go via Fresno Yosemite International, which provides access from the south. Coming from San Francisco, you will enter the park from one of the several west entrances. Yosemite has wild mountain weather from the maritime systems that roll in from the coast. You can have rain, hot and dry weather, and afternoon thunderstorms in the peak season. In this large park, you will have multiple campgrounds to choose from—from backcountry to full service. Look into High Sierra Camps, spaced on a loop trail in Yosemite's high country. Hike to canvas tent cabins, complete with mattresses, blankets, hot showers, and restrooms. Several lodges and inns are in the park and in nearby communities.

Ten More National Parks and National Seashores

The preceding national parks are some of the most popular because of their rugged beauty, unique natural history, and broad range of recreational activities. This second group consists of primarily water-based parks or those that have beautiful beaches. They are scattered across the U.S., so you won't have to travel too far to find one. Some offer primarily beach camping for tidepooling, surfing, windsurfing, snorkeling, diving, or swimming. A few are accessible primarily by canoe, kayak, dory, sailboat, or motorboat, where permitted.

These might not have the bold, rugged scenery of the mountain- or desert-based parks. But they are still strong on scenery and solace, have loads of wildlife and waterfowl, offer a multitude of family activities, and come with clean, crisp sea air 24/7 at no extra cost.

Except for a few, you don't necessarily need watercraft for these parks. You can camp on the beach, take a boat tour or shuttle where needed, or rent a paddle boat or canoe. There are plenty of hiking and biking trails, too, most of which are accessible by car. National seashores are managed by the National Park Service, so they have most of the amenities of the parks, like ranger stations, visitors centers, and campgrounds. Often the campgrounds are less developed and less numerous. One, Cape Cod, has no camping in the park.

Also of note, the national seashores are frequently located near major metropolitan areas. Thus, you can combine an adventure trip with a trip to a city. Cape Cod is near Boston, for example. The Canaveral National Seashore is near the space center in Orlando. Point Reyes is near San Francisco. Couple a week of camping with a few days of culture, shopping, or science in the city. Check www.nps.gov for the scoop on these national parks and seashores.

Tidepooling on the coast is a squishy and smelly experience.

1. ACADIA

The first national park east of the Mississippi River, Acadia is way up in the northeast corner of the U.S. and well worth the trek. Granite-domed mountains, thick woods, and a multitude of lakes are punctuated by a rugged Atlantic shoreline. People lived here some 5,000 years ago, so in addition to wildlife and waterfowl, the cultural history is rich. The Islesford Historical Museum has exhibits on ship trade, navigation aids, old photographs, and tools. You can walk, hike, trek, or bike 115 miles of old carriage roads with ocean and forest views. Hike trails or paddle around the seashore in canoe or kayak.

You can book a flight into Hancock County Airport, about ten miles from Acadia, or Bangor International Airport, about one hour away. Alternatively, drive six hours north of Boston by car. You will likely have many sunny days in summer, with mild to cool temperatures in this maritime climate. The rather brisk fall is punctuated by the brilliant colors of New England's changing leaves. Rain and fog can occur nearly anytime, so bring a raincoat and boots. Most of the campgrounds are open all year. You can choose one on the seashore or in the famous Maine woods.

2. CAPE HATTERAS NATIONAL SEASHORE

Seventy miles of barrier islands provide a variety of recreational and historical opportunities at this mid-Atlantic seashore. For birders, Cape Hatteras is the wintering grounds for many migrating waterfowl. In addition, you will find premier windsurfing, surfing, and fishing along the cape. Treacherous currents, shoals, and storms have given it the moniker "Graveyard of the Atlantic." Shipwrecks, lighthouses, and the U.S. Lifesaving Service all have a fascinating history here. Check out the "Especially for Kids" program at visitors centers; it includes art projects, pirate stories, campfire tales on the beach, fishing with a ranger, and turtle talks.

Fly into Norfolk, Virginia, about a hundred miles away, or Raleigh-Durham, North Carolina, about two hundred miles away. State-operated toll ferries give access to the seashore, as do bridges. This seaside climate is windy and cool year-round. Sometimes strong storm winds pummel the coast; otherwise, gentle sea breezes smooth out the summer heat and humidity. Thunderstorms and mosquitoes can mar otherwise pleasant days on this coast. Choose from a variety of campgrounds with full facilities. Lodging in local communities includes a range of hotels, inns, and B&Bs.

3. CAPE COD NATIONAL SEASHORE

Nearly forty miles of pristine beaches have been set aside on an otherwise crowded peninsula. Cape Cod boasts clear, deep kettle ponds, long beaches, mellow surf, and historic structures, including a lighthouse, a lifesaving station, and several homesteads. The Salt Pond Visitors Center has exhibits on salt marsh plants and animals, beach ecosystems, and residential and migratory birds. The Nauset Marsh and Buttonbush trails are short interpretive paths. Province Lands Visitors Center has an observation deck with a view of dunes, beach, ocean, and historic buildings. It also has an exhibit on the Pilgrims' landing in Provincetown. If swimming, self-guided nature trails, and scenic picnics haven't filled up your day, check out ranger-led canoe tours and surfcasting and shellfishing demonstrations. Or ride one of three paved bike trails in the park or the Cape Cod Rail Trail bike trail just outside the park.

Fly into Boston's Logan Airport, then take a commuter flight to Hyannis or Provincetown. Alternatively, make the short drive up from Boston. Like many Atlantic beaches, Cape Cod can have cool, wet weather in spring and fall but many warm, sunny summer days. It is almost always cool at night, especially with a sea breeze. Cape Cod has no campgrounds in the park; it is a day-use area only. However, Nickerson State Park and private campgrounds are nearby. Lodging is abundant in nearby inns, hotels, or RV parks.

It's great to be a kid at the beach.

4. EVERGLADES

Everglades is the only subtropical preserve in America. Sawgrass prairies, mangrove and cypress swamps, pinelands and hardwood hammocks, and estuarine environments give this large park a rather unique feel. The huge wading bird population includes roseate spoonbill, wood stork, great blue heron, and egrets. Plus, this is the only place in the world where alligators and crocodiles coexist. The Flamingo Visitors Center is the starting point for many hiking and canoe trails. The Gulf Coast Visitors Center is the gateway to Ten Thousand Islands, a maze of mangrove islands and waterways. Tram tours from Shark Valley Visitors Center can be fun too.

Fly into Miami, Fort Lauderdale, or Fort Myers airports in South Florida. Warm and humid weather is the year-round norm. Summers can be rather hot and humid, with temperatures over 90. Thunderstorms and mosquitoes are problematic in evenings. Hurricanes are possible June to November. Campgrounds and Flamingo Lodge can fill up in the busy season.

5. CANAVERAL NATIONAL SEASHORE

Located near Titusville and New Smyrna Beach, Florida, on a barrier island, Canaveral has ocean, beach, dune, hammock, lagoon, salt marsh, and pine flatland habitats. Numerous endangered species live here, including logger-head, green, and leatherback sea turtles, West Indian manatee, southern

Who needs pants? Aloof on the beach.

bald eagle, wood stork, peregrine falcon, eastern indigo snake, and Florida scrub jay. It is fun to have small boats or canoes to visit the islands. Visitors center displays include info on sea turtle nesting and hatching and Timucuan Indian artifacts. There are several cultural exhibits such as Eldora State House Museum, which highlights early settlers, and Mosquito Lagoon House of Refuge, an old shipwreck shelter.

Reach the seashore via Orlando International Airport. Like other spots in Florida, weather tends to be either warm and humid or hot and humid. Afternoons bring thunderstorms, and evenings bring mosquitoes. Generally, the weather can be milder and drier in winter. There is year-round beach or island camping. Be advised that beaches can be closed for sea turtle nesting season in summer.

6. HALEAKALA
Maui's luscious national park combines two rather distinct ecosystems: The active volcano Haleakala stands 10,023 feet high, and the famed Kipahulu coast near Hana is a luscious tropical wonderland. The two are not connected directly. Visitors centers are located at the park entrance and summit of Haleakala, with exhibits on natural, geological, and cultural heritage. A separate visitors center is located in the Kipahulu region. Check out sky-

watching: clouds, surf, views, rainbows, moonbows, hallows, planets, and stars. Or take your family on a Hawaiian cultural hike.

Fly into Kahului, Maui's airport. Weather is distinct for the two sections of the park. On the Haleakala, temperatures can be cool, and sometimes snow caps the summit. On the Kipahulu coast, warm temperatures typical of Hawaii can be punctuated with clouds, rain, and winds. There are a few small primitive campgrounds and some backcountry campsites. A few wilderness cabins are accessed by a four-mile hike.

7. ISLE ROYALE

Located near Houghton, Michigan, these wild North Woods sport wolves and moose, cool and dramatic weather, clear water, and the rugged coastline of Lake Superior. This archipelago, nine miles wide and forty-five miles long, was formed from ancient lava flows. The park includes 165 miles of trails and thirty-six campgrounds ideal for boaters and paddlers. Explore shipwrecks, lighthouses, copper mines, and a commercial fishery. This park is accessible only by boat or float plane.

The main entrances and parking areas are Houghton and Copper Harbor in Michigan and Grand Portage, Minnesota. Ferries provide access to Isle Royale, as do seaplane services. Rock Harbor Lodge offers the M.V. *Sandy*, a vessel which gives tours. Water taxis as well as boat and canoe rentals are available. Because it's on Lake Superior, cool, windy weather is the norm. Dense fog, sun, thunderstorms, and rain can occur anytime. Bring warm wind- and waterproof clothing. Unlike other parks, these seasonal campgrounds limit campers from two to five nights. These primitive tent sites sometimes have shelters. Rock Harbor Lodge offers the only accommodations.

8. PADRE ISLAND NATIONAL SEASHORE

Near Corpus Christi, Texas, Padre Island is the longest undeveloped barrier island in the world. The endless beaches boast abundant recreation: surfcasting, surfing, windsurfing, kiteboarding, kiting, or biking. In addition, you may get a chance to see baby sea turtles. Located on North Padre Island, the park is open all year.

Corpus Christi International is the closest airport. Typical of the Gulf Coast, Padre Island weather is warm and humid. Nights are warm, even in winter. Gentle thermal winds are present nearly every day. Primitive and semiprimitive camping is located on the beach or in the dunes. Unique to this park, you can camp directly on North Beach. With no specific campsites, there is always space.

9. POINT REYES NATIONAL SEASHORE

Located close to the San Francisco Bay, Point Reyes is home to the spectacular scenery of ocean shore break, grasslands, hillsides, and forests typical of pre-developed California. Smack in the middle of California, you will find dozens of marine mammals and birds, ranging from elk to elephant seals. This is one of the best spots to view migrating California gray whales. Check out Bear Valley Visitors Center, which has exhibits on diverse ecosystems and cultural heritage. The weather station has a seismograph and touch table. The Lighthouse Visitors Center has whale, wildflower, bird, and maritime history exhibits. You can walk the lighthouse stairs and visit the lens room to see the original clockworks and 130-year-old Fresnel lens.

Fly into San Francisco International or Oakland Airport; Point Reyes is about thirty-five miles north of San Francisco on scenic Highway 1. Typically, you will find warm, dry summers and cool, rainy weather the rest of the year. Mild winds are nearly constant due to exposed headland and beaches. Also, fog is common in summer and early fall. Four backpacking or bicycle access campgrounds are located here. Coast Camp is the shortest hike at 1.8 miles from car to campground; it also has easy beach access. Boat-in camping is possible on the beach at Tomales Bay. The only lodge is Hostelling International-Point Reyes, with dorm-style rooms and one family room.

10. VOYAGEURS

In the southern Canadian Shield, Voyageurs has some of the oldest exposed rock in the world. Rolling hills, bogs, beaver dams, swamps, islands, and lakes punctuate this glacier-carved land. The famed North Woods boreal ecosystem is rich with wildlife. The park's cultural heritage begins with the voyageurs, French-Canadian explorers that traveled via birch-bark canoes. Located in the northern Minnesota lakes district, this water-based park is accessed via watercraft via the Kabetogama peninsula. Check out the "River of Lakes, Roads of Ice" exhibit, which explores natural and cultural history of transportation and the fur trade.

To get to Voyageurs, fly into Minneapolis–St. Paul, about three hundred miles away. Take a commuter flight to International Falls or Hibbing Airport, near the park. Temperatures are usually cool and continental, with warm but short summers. The park has many boat-accessed campgrounds, up to 215 sites on the four large lakes. Most are set up for tent camping or houseboat mooring. Kettle Falls Hotel is open in summer.

15

Ten Family-Friendly Winter Resorts and Mountain Towns

All kids love a winter vacation, especially if they get to take time off school. Many families pick a ski resort and head to the same place every year. Others like to visit a new place every year or two. When my kids were young, we went to the same ski hill every year for a week with the extended family, including cousins and grandparents. This gave my kids a chance to get to know a winter resort away from home. We also tried to take at least one trip to a new place every year too. This keeps our winter ski and snowboard vacations new and exciting. Not every family can afford to do multiple winter resort trips every year, so here's a synopsis of some of the better resorts for families.

What to look for in a resort? There should be lots of family-friendly features. I like lodges close to the hill that won't cost you a month's salary, a variety of terrain from beginner to expert, good family restaurants, and a location close to an airport with a good shuttle system, for starters. Also, there should be excellent day care and a ski school, lots of activities for kids and families, and a small walking village with extras like an ice skating rink, cinema, or toy store. It's a bonus if you don't have to get in the car the whole week. It's also nice to have alternative activities besides skiing and snowboarding, like cross-country skiing, snowshoeing, or ice skating, for family members who don't slide.

If you want to look for value, here are some helpful hints. Avoid Christmas and Presidents' Day weekend. Sneak in a trip before Christmas, in early January, or during spring break. Search for packages that let kids fly, stay, and ski for free. Look for all-inclusive lodging and lift tickets for the best deals. Shop around. If off-slope lodging is significantly cheaper than slopeside, often the resort has a free shuttle to the ski lifts.

Busting through the gate, kids learn at ski camp.

Keep in mind, many of these mountain towns and resorts are great vacations for spring, summer, or fall too. Once the snow melts, you'll find biking and hiking trails, fishing holes, swimming pools, and other family activities. In fall and spring, you can find uncrowded lodges and better prices. Warm days and cool nights provide great temperatures for viewing beautiful spring flowers or fall leaves.

1. THE BEST FAMILY RESORT EVER: SMUGGLERS' NOTCH, VERMONT

Smugglers' Notch, nestled in Vermont's Green Mountains, has the family market dialed. In fact, it's the resort all others are compared to for family fun. Check out the Daily Cookie Race for kids where everyone wins, the Mogul Mouse snow mascot, or the Science of Nature program, which includes the likes of Professor Alpine and the Wacky Wizard snow demo.

Après-ski, you will find winter fire sing-alongs, karaoke, tubing, hot tubs, and ice skating. Treasures, the new day care, has state-of-the-art amenities like heated floors, giant fish tanks, pint-sized toilets and sinks, a 5,400-square-foot rumpus room, a one-way parental spying mirror, heated walkways, and a first aid–trained staff. Did they forget anything? Kids' night out focuses on activities like crafts, fireworks, and movies. Little guys will love the Fun Zone play area. Two teen centers provide internet computers, video games, music, and a soda bar. Teen Alley, focused on younger teens, has a Snow Deck Park. Outer Limits is for kids ages sixteen and above. You can find Smugglers' Notch on the web at www.smuggs.com.

Alternatively, try Okemo, Vermont, a cozy family-owned resort oozing hospitality. The mountain features gentle terrain and guided snowshoe trails. Newly expanded, Jackson Gore peak area provides more advanced trails. The Penguin Playground day care and ski school center are not too expensive. During evenings, look into kids' night out or the Rampage Teen Center with indoor skate park. Let your kids log on to Kids Club Snowmonsters before you go (www.okemo.com).

Another Northeast family-friendly resort, Sugarloaf, Maine, has a compact base village tucked below a large versatile ski area. A large indoor skate bowl called Antigravity Complex also includes trampolines, a rock climbing wall, sport court, running track, weights, and aerobics. Turbo Tubing with a handle tow gives nonskiers an alternative adrenaline rush. Evening activities include games, movies, and Families in Motion for skating and sledding. Sugarloaf's website is www.sugarloaf.com.

2. BIGGER IS SOMETIMES BETTER: KILLINGTON, VERMONT

Killington is huge, and it has long been favored by families that have a broad range of skiers. Long groomers are great for speed seekers or intermediates. Steeps and trees are great for adventurers. Parks and pipes are for kids who like to twist, turn, and catch air. The large resort is matched by grandiose facilities, lots of lodging, and reasonable packages. Extensive snowmaking takes some stress out of the vacation: You'll probably always have decent snow. Teens and young adults will like the Ram's Head Family Center. Parents will like the Friendly Penguin Daycare Center or one of the several learn-to-ski programs for kids. Killington Road village area has shops, nightspots, food, and dining. Log on to www.killington.com.

For a more low-key experience, look into Bretton Woods, New Hampshire (www.brettonwoods.com). The recently expanded resort puts kids and families first. A family learning center has a new quad chair, is free, and there are lots of affordable motels. A full sports center has a pool as well as other après-ski activities. On weekends, look for magicians, clowns, games, and sledding. Check out the historic Mount Washington Hotel for a real treat.

3. BEST IN THE MIDWEST: BOYNE MOUNTAIN, MICHIGAN

Frequently rated best in the Midwest by the national magazines, Boyne Mountain (www.boynemountain.com) is one of the largest resorts in this area. Plenty of groomed trails and a variety of beginner and intermediate terrain provide something for everyone. Slopeside, there are twelve lifts and a six-person quad. For snowboarders and skiers, check out the terrain parks and half pipes. Try night skiing, tubing, ice skating, snowshoeing, or cross-country skiing. A village offers lots of shopping and food.

4. THE HISTORIC WEST: STEAMBOAT, COLORADO

One of the original mining-towns-turned-ski-hills, Steamboat is another family-friendly winter resort. They have one of the original "kids ski free" programs (free under age twelve with a five-day parent ticket). Olympic gold medalist Billy Kidd will give your whole family a mountain tour. Steamboat takes an individual approach to ski school: It attempts to keep the same instructor with your kids for an entire week. Advanced teens and parents can get first tracks at opening every morning. There is a free shuttle downtown, or in nice weather, you can walk. You'll find a full range of lodging and lots of shopping and family restaurants. They are online at www.steamboat.com.

Also check out Telluride, Colorado (www.tellurideskiresort.com). The historic mining town is now replete with development and glitz. The Telluride Mountain Village Activity Center is the hub for family fun, albeit a bit removed from town. Families can ride, glide, or slide at Kids' Zone or Trill Hill on tubes, skiskates, and skibikes. The Sprite Air Garden Terrain Park or Nordic center satisfies both your jibbing snowboarder and your mellow cross-country skier. Evenings in the Plaza Arcade keep your kids entertained with video, pinball, air hockey, and foosball games.

5. CLASSIC COLORADO: ASPEN/SNOWMASS, COLORADO

The flagship resort may be Aspen for the upscale experience. Four ski resorts in one, Aspen Highlands and Aspen Mountain are more for experts, and Snowmass and Buttermilk are for all abilities (www.aspensnowmass.com). Check out Crazy Train, one of the longest terrain parks ever. Or head straight to Family Zone, which is a conglomerate of adventure trails, children's race areas with practice gates, picnic spots, terrain parks, half pipes, and an interactive tree trail. At Buttermilk, Fort Frog is an educational play area. Check out snowcat or dogsled rides, ice skating, or the skate park.

You can find a multitude of winter resorts serviced out of Denver. Try Winter Park, Colorado, the city of Denver–owned resort, for a more low-key experience. It has a superb ski school, day care, and disabled ski program. A variety of beginner and intermediate terrain is supplemented with a special novice area. Be advised, this place is so cool it can get crowded. You can find it online at www.winterpark.com.

Wait until they are teenagers to wolf pack on the ski hill.

Breckenridge, Colorado, is huge, but six-person chairs take loads of people up the mountain. For kids, Café Breck is open evenings. Bring the whole crew or drop off the kids at BASH: Breckenridge After Ski/Snowboard Hangout; you'll leave them with professional supervision and arts, games, or other activities. It's also one of the Burton Learn to Ride centers for snowboarding. Learn more at www.breckenridge.com.

Or try Copper Mountain, Colorado (www.ski-copper.com). Its new base center is fully family-friendly. The Sled Shed shuttles kids to ski and snowboard lessons. Kids will groove at the Schoolhouse day care, with kid-sized restrooms and cafeteria tables and a giant slide from second floor to ground level. On the hill, find the kids' adventure trail. Lessons end early for parents who want to take a few runs with the little shredders (or book them for after-ski-school Kids' Camp). Kids' night out has evening programs with games, videos, and art, and it's free if you dine at Copper.

6. STEEP AND DEEP: JACKSON HOLE, WYOMING

Come here for the skiing only. This huge resort boasts steep terrain and loads of deep powder. But there's plenty of intermediate terrain too—the same as an entire small resort. Slopeside lodging is more expensive, so look

One on the hill, one on the back: A parent teaches both the thrill.

for lodging in the town of Jackson, twenty minutes away. A public bus system will shuttle you to the mountain alongside the locals. For kids, check out Jackson Hole Kids' Ranch and Team Extreme. Younger ones might like Fort Wyoming, a western sports playground, or Ske-Cology, an interactive environmental program that promotes environmental education with skiing. Don't want to ski for a day? Teton National Park and National Elk Refuge is minutes from Jackson. Visit www.jacksonhole.com.

For more intermediate terrain, less expense, and arguably better snow, look at Grand Targhee, Wyoming (www.grandtarghee.com). The self-contained central base area makes the mountain manageable. Kids under fourteen ski free, and there are virtually no crowds, ever. The Powder Scouts teach kids to cruise groomed runs and cut up powder. Grand Targhee has a kids' trail map, so they can view the resort map on their terms. With kids you will probably want slopeside lodging, since the resort is a bit isolated from the town of Driggs, Idaho.

If you want to ski Utah, home of the famed greatest snow on earth, Snowbird is the place for advanced skiing. Families with intermediate and beginner skiers and snowboarders will like Solitude or The Canyons in nearby Park City.

7. THE PLACE IT ALL STARTED: SUN VALLEY, IDAHO

The first destination winter resort in the U.S. was founded in 1935 by Count Felix Schaffgtosch when he sought out a ski town along the rail line. Sun Valley is jam-packed with intermediate runs and almost entirely serviced snowmaking. You probably will miss the few days of powder that come here, but count on sun and manufactured snow. Ketchem, Idaho, is another western town gone glitz, so search out family restaurants and budget activities. You'll find less expensive lodging in Ketchem, so plan to take the public bus to the slopes if you don't have a car. Don't forget to ice skate at the Sun Valley Lodge and sit through Sun Valley Serenade at the Opera House. Find out more at www.sunvalley.com.

For a more economical northern Rocky Mountain resort, try Big Mountain, Montana. It doesn't have the sun (try fog) or the snowmaking capacity of Sun Valley, but it's a working-class western town and a family-friendly resort to boot. In fact, one lift is entirely free. If you live along the rail line, take Amtrak. Visit www.bigmtn.com for the scoop.

8. CALIFORNIA'S SIERRA: NORTHSTAR-AT-TAHOE, CALIFORNIA

There's a ton of great skiing at Lake Tahoe and numerous resorts. Families love Northstar. All runs drop into the central base village, and a gondola heads up the midmountain ski-school area. Ski-school ages overlap, so your kid will be in a group with similar skills, not ages. Also, the Parent Predicament Ticket can be shared between two parents. Mom spends the morning with the little guys while dad rips with friends. Then mom and dad switch on the same ticket in the afternoon. You'll find plenty of family lodging, free shuttles, and Polaris Park with snowbikes and other toys. Log onto www.northstarattahoe.com.

Want to go to Tahoe and find more challenge? Don't miss Squaw Valley (www.squaw.com). This birthplace of extreme skiing was also the site of the 1968 Winter Olympics. It has huge terrain, lots of kids' programs, and slopeside lodging. You will find crowds on long weekends. Check out ice skating, rock climbing, and the swimming pool.

9. YEAR-ROUND: TIMBERLINE, OREGON

Timberline's year-round snow is something of an anomaly. Although the winter can sometimes be lackluster, masses of preteens and teens head for T-line for the summer camps on the permanently snow-covered Palmer Glacier. They train alongside the U.S. Ski Team and many other national ski teams. Based in Government Camp, or Govy, this is quite a scene in mid-July. The mountain is open in the morning, leaving plenty of time in the afternoon to hang out in the skate park, practice dry land training, or head down to Hood River for windsurfing, kiteboarding, mountain biking, or kayaking. Beware, your kids may want you to stay at home.

Also try Mount Bachelor, Oregon, central Oregon's high desert volcanic ski area (www.mtbachelor.com). The entire volcano is the resort. There is terrain for everyone, including treed glades and above-treeline bowls. The vistas are scenic, and the snow is quality. You won't find any slopeside lodging here, though, which is why this mountain is still wild. Stay in Bend or Sunriver, which are twenty minutes away.

10. UP NORTH: WHISTLER/BLACKCOMB, BRITISH COLUMBIA

Whistler and Blackcomb are separate resorts, yet they are connected by one common base village. You can't ski both Whistler and Blackcomb in a day—they are too huge. Even when the weather is poor down low, you can find epic days in powder and sun up top. The real plus is the European-style base village with pedestrian streets. Although some of the newer lodging facilities are separate from the main village, it is still a compact town. Ski the top half of Blackcomb for more advanced runs, or stay on Whistler with the whole family. You will find plenty of adventure for kids. Teens will love the après-ski scene in the village. Find out more at www.whistler-blackcomb.com.

Canada has some wonderful family-style resorts scattered across its southwestern corner. Big White in Kelowna, B.C., has night or heli-skiing, a mini-snowmobile track for kids, and sleigh rides. Whitewater in Nelson, B.C., has terrain for all levels, including cruisers, trees, steeps, deeps, and beginner-only areas. Fernie Ski Valley in Fernie, Alberta, has a bit better snow, but it can be harder to get to.

16

Ten Trips of a Lifetime

A trip of a lifetime can mean many things to different families. Sometimes it means mom and dad take an entire month off work. Take your family on a long backpacking trip, sailing adventure, or drive across the United States to visit several national parks. Save up for a Christmas trip to ski Europe. Hike the Inca Trail to the famed Machu Picchu in Peru or the sail to the Galapagos Islands in Ecuador. Whatever the case, these trips take lots of planning and preparation, sometimes several years' worth. They can be logistically challenging, but the rewards are fabulous.

The fact is, you don't have to have a huge budget to do some lifetime trips, but you do have to have time off from work. Some can be completed in two to three weeks, but more time is usually better. My best advice: Put some money away in a vacation fund, save up frequent flier miles and vacation days, and plan several years ahead.

I'll give you my extreme compulsive example: When my kids were one and three years old, I signed up on the twelve-year waiting list for a private raft permit down the Colorado River through the Grand Canyon. Anyone can go on short notice if you pay for a commercial trip. But a private trip means I will invite eighteen friends down the river in a course of three weeks. We can bring lots of friends, plan campsites and side hikes, and do some serious bonding amidst the great rapids. At the time I signed up on the list, the wait was ten to twelve years for a permit. My kids will be in their early teens when my number comes up, the perfect age for an epic trip.

Here are some selected trips that will give you ideas. These are some widely recognized trips that are great for families, but be creative. You can do any variation of these trips or use them as a basis to start your own list.

1. GO LONG-DISTANCE BACKPACKING

There are several trails in the U.S. that are called long-distance hikes because they are long, months long, not to mention incredibly scenic. There are three well-known long-distance trails. The Pacific Crest Trail goes from Mexico to Canada through California, Oregon, and Washington. It runs right up the spine of the Sierra Nevada Mountains and then through the Northwest's Cascade Mountains. It takes about six months to hike. The Appalachian Trail runs from Georgia to Maine's Mount Katahdin and is a bit shorter. The Continental Divide traverses the Rocky Mountains from Mexico to Canada. The Pacific Crest and Appalachian trails have a network for through hikers. You can send yourself resupply boxes to post offices along the way and even catch a motel room at various towns that the trails pass through.

But don't be overwhelmed; you don't have to hike the whole trail. One friend of mine took her kids (ages nine, eleven, and thirteen) on a five-week hike on the northern Oregon section of the Pacific Crest. Another outdoor author wrote a book about taking her kids down the length of the Continental Divide over the course of five summers using bikes and llamas for support. In a pinch, pick two weeks and hike the most scenic section of any one of these trails.

2. BIKE ACROSS AMERICA

Biking is an all-American pastime. And biking across America is something many outdoor adventurers have on their tick list. You can bike the whole way over many months, choosing one of several routes. Many cyclists ride in the summer along the northern U.S. for the best combination of mild temperatures and sunny weather.

Alternatively, pick one or two states to ride through. Ride from campground to campground or even motel to motel. One family friend took his kids from Milwaukee to West Glacier, Montana, over the course of six weeks using a tandem bike for his ten-year-old. Another colleague is planning a trip from New York to Oregon, leaving the first day of summer break and returning the week before school starts. She promised her teenage daughter she could have a shower in a motel or campground at least every third day.

3. VISIT BAJA, MEXICO

Baja is a wonderful, safe, fantastic adventure that will give your family a glimpse at pristine beaches, rugged uncrowded mountains, and friendly people. A bonus is that if you tour "the Baja" with your own vehicle, it can be an inexpensive trip that is strong on great experiences. And Baja is a multisport wonderland.

Kayak the Vermillion Sea from San Felipe to Cabo San Lucas over several months. Or take a surf trip down the west coast, ending up in famed Todos Santos, one of the best surf breaks in the world. Around the Cabo San Lucas cape area on the southern tip, you can surf, windsurf, dive, sail, kayak, snorkel, or beach hike. Right down the middle of the peninsula you'll find rugged mountain trails and well-preserved historic missions.

The Baja can be driven in as little as one week from California, but that's a lot of car time. Either spend a month, or consider driving one way with your kids and letting them fly back with your spouse.

4. RAFT THE GRAND CANYON

Float through tranquil plunge pools, ride huge rapids, hike in ancient geology, camp on pristine beaches, and have a ball on the river with family and friends. Rafting the Colorado River through the Grand Canyon is an epic trip of a lifetime: thrilling, educational, interactive, and beautiful. There are family-friendly campsites, warm nights, few insects, and family-oriented river companies that emphasize safety. It can be as strenuous or as relaxing as you want it to be.

To raft the full canyon, put in at Lees Ferry and take out at Diamond Ferry. The trip takes fourteen to eighteen days. While on the river, you'll experience a wild adrenaline ride on the 240 major rapids. When floating through tranquil stretches, you can paddle a kayak; fish for brook, rainbow, or cutthroat trout; or listen to your guide talk about the flora, fauna, and ancient geology. When in camp, explore slot canyons, waterfalls, spectacular vistas, natural arches, and caves. Or write in a journal.

If you can only spare a week or so, you can take a six- or nine-day trip. Phantom Ranch is the halfway point on the river, a one-day hike on the Bright Angel Trail to or from the South Rim Village. You can join a trip in progress to raft the lower half.

5. SKI AND SNOWBOARD EUROPE'S ALPS

A ski trip to Europe is a favorite among outdoor families. You can stick to one of the many family-friendly ski towns across eastern France, Switzerland, Austria, or northern Italy. Families with school-age kids will adore the quintessential European ski villages of the Arlberg region in Austria. This includes the famed twin towns of Lech and Zurs and the lower key villages of St. Anton, St. Christoph, and Stuben. You'll find tons of skiing and snowboarding here, loads of family activities, and a long history of rich alpine culture. Families with teens who are expert skiers or climbers may want to search out extreme-sports central at Chamonix-Mont-Blanc, France. If you want to visit Switzerland, St. Moritz is at the apex of the skiing life, but it is somewhat pricey. Try Davos or Klosters for a more low-key experience. For an Italian trip, check out Cortina d'Ampezzo, site of the 1956 Winter Olympics, or Val Gardena, nestled in the Dolomites. Italy is another great family haunt because of world-class skiing and good prices. Plus you can spend a few days in Florence or Venice.

For a special treat, take a European ski trip during Christmas. Your kids will get a chance to experience the rich culture that is much less commercial than it is in America. You may have to search out deals and pick out-of-the-way places to avoid crowds.

If your kids are older and have backcountry skiing or snowboarding experience, you may want to attempt the famed Haute Route. This is the most famous overland ski trail that takes you from Chamonix, France, home of Mont Blanc, to Zermatt, Switzerland, and the Matterhorn. You can ski the high traverse over the course of a week. Travel from inn to inn, while your guide service shuttles your gear and provides food along the way.

6. SAIL THE INSIDE PASSAGE TO ALASKA

Sailing is a sport beloved by families. If you don't sail, you might like renting a motor yacht or signing up for an educational cruise. Although many families love the fair weather of the Caribbean or easy access of the Atlantic seaboard, the Inside Passage, the major waterway that runs from the Puget Sound in Washington up to Anchorage, Alaska, is one of the most beautiful and rugged boat trips.

The Inside Passage is protected from the rough North Pacific by Vancouver Island and an archipelago along the Pacific Coast of British Columbia and the Alaska peninsula. The passage is a major commercial fishing route to get to the Alaskan fishing grounds, as well as a thoroughfare for recreational cruisers, paddlers, and sailors. You'll float next to orca pods and green islands jam-packed with old-growth Douglas fir, western red cedar, and hemlock. Watch for bears, bald eagles, and wolves, and fish for gigantic salmon.

There are many ways to visit the sixteen-hundred-mile Inside Passage. You can take a commercial cruise, sail your own boat, or ride the Alaska Marine Highway, the state ferry system that will take cars, RVs, foot passengers, and even kayakers with their boats. Friends have kayaked this whole trip one-way. You can resupply at towns along the way, but they are far between.

7. TAKE A GUIDED ADVENTURE OVERSEAS

Guided adventures are a great way to see a remote and fascinating part of the world without having to spend a lot of time and energy planning a trip.

Guided trips take out a lot of the uncertainty: Will the hotel be suitable for kids? Will we eat food we like? How will we get to and from the airport? You can surf the internet and find myriad adventure travel outfitters. You might first pick your location and then find a family-friendly guide service. Alternatively, search the website of a family-oriented outfitter and choose from a dozen package tours.

There are lots of favorite trips that combine adventure sports and travel with natural and cultural history. Most of these are geared for older kids. Fortunately, you can make these trips as easy or as strenuous as you choose.

For exotic trips, check out the Galapagos Islands via a motor yacht or sailboat. Snorkel, swim, or kayak in Darwin's "little world within itself" alongside sea turtles, penguins, and sea lions. Hike on Peru's Inca Trail to the well-preserved ancient city of Machu Picchu. Check out Tanzania's famous Serengeti National Park in Africa. Wildlife treks via four-wheel-drive SUVs will have you dining in style and sleeping in large wood-floor tents. Visit Ngorongoro Crater or add in a climb of Mount Kilimanjaro. Nepal trekking is fabulous for families too. You will hike among the rice and mustard fields and rhododendron and oak forests between lodges. Scenic vistas are coupled with friendly people. For a multisport adventure, try Costa Rica. Hike the national parks, trek in jungles, raft whitewater, or surf some of the best waves of your life.

You don't have to pick such exotic locales, though. Many outfitters organize bike tours of Europe or New England, wildlife tours in Alaska, kayak or scuba trips in the Caribbean, adventures in Mexico, or ski and snowboard vacations.

8. DO IT ALL IN NEW ZEALAND

There's a reason New Zealand's South Island, and Queenstown in particular, is known as the "adventure capital of the world." Bungee jumping, one of the original thrill sports, started here. You'll have so much to do here, you'll either need to focus on one adventure or stay at least a month. The abundant recreational opportunities are punctuated by a lack of crowds and towns chock-full of smiling people. You'll find tons of local outfitters and lots of nice places to stay.

Ski and snowboard out of Queenstown or Wanaka, alpine towns with access to Coronet Peak and Remarkables winter resorts. Climb in the southern Alps, the training grounds for Everest summiteer Edmund Hillary. Climb the glacial-clad volcanoes of Mount Cook and Mount Aspring. Backpack the world-famous Milford or Routeburn tracks. Kayak in the Fjordlands National Park. Surf the Waikato Coast, Whale Bay, or Manu Bay. Have more energy? Try ballooning, canyoning, caving, whitewater rafting, wind-surfing, snorkeling, or diving. The list goes on and on.

9. CLIMB A MOUNTAIN

With older kids, especially those about to head off to college, climbing a mountain can be a wonderful experience. The rugged beauty of the high alpine world and the physical challenge of climbing can provide the back-drop for wonderful bonding time. Remember, climbing mountains is risky, but it does not have to be highly technical or extremely hazardous. Some favorite peaks of mine include the snow-clad volcanoes in the Pacific North-west's Cascade Range, granite domes of California's Sierra Nevada, Col-orado's Fourteeners (peaks over 14,000 feet high), or Wyoming's Tetons. But you may have mountains near your home only 4,000 feet high that will serve just as well. Spend a night in a tent, climb to the peak at sunrise, and enjoy the solitude of an age-old adventure. If you're not experienced, enroll yourself and your child in a climbing school.

10. LEARN A NEW SPORT

A lifetime trip doesn't necessarily have to be far away from home in a remote part of the world, and it doesn't have to break your bank. One of the best and most rewarding trips is to learn a new sport with your children. You might try something you've always dreamed about. Alternatively, pick up a sport that your son or daughter chooses. This is a chance to take up a new sport with your older child. Also, it will give you a great excuse to plan trips with your child, even after he or she leaves the house.

You can start with a local class; then work on skills on short day or weekend trips close to home. And finally, reward yourself with a trip where you can practice. It can range from skiing or snowboarding to water sports like scuba diving, surfing, or windsurfing. It may even be something as sim-ple as cycling. Get road bikes and ride on a regular basis. Once you've taken many local biking trips, plan a cycling trip to Europe and watch part of the Tour de France.

Part 4

SAFETY

Parents always ask me about safety issues when adventuring with children. It's okay to be concerned. When you head outdoors into the wilds with your children, they will most likely get bruised and cut. They will sprain ankles. They will get too cold or too hot. They will get hungry, thirsty, and tired. Hopefully, with close supervision, you can keep injuries and illnesses to a minimum and address concerns, especially preventable problems, quickly.

These final two chapters are designed to give you a broad overview to common outdoor sports and adventure travel health issues. They will help you design a first aid kit for outings. With proper supervision, close attention to wounds and illness, and checking in with your doctor, you should be able to handle most injuries and illnesses. Remember, these chapters are only designed to give you a broad overview and an introduction to the topic. They will not substitute for formal training in first aid or medical care in the backcountry. You should get a good outdoor first aid kit and learn how to use it. Consider a course on outdoor first aid. Get a good book on the techniques to supplement your class. Also, check with your doctor before you go and if your child gets sick or injured.

17

First Aid for Families and First Aid Kits

When you head into the wilds with kids in tow, you should have a basic first aid kit and know how to use it. Often, the American Red Cross or your local community college will have first aid courses. It's also a good idea to take a cardiopulmonary resuscitation course designed for adults and kids, sometimes called a "Small Hearts" CPR course. You'll probably never need it, but if you do, you can save your child's or an adult's life. It also helps to read a first aid book and have a pocket first aid pamphlet in your first aid kit.

Before you head out on an adventure, always make sure your kids are healthy. If they are the least bit ill, you won't have fun and they won't have fun. As parents, we don't like doing much of anything when we are sick, so don't make your kids travel sick, no matter how long you planned or how much effort it took to pack. It's not fair to your children: It could worsen their health, and you might turn them off to outdoor sports or adventures.

COMMON MEDICAL ISSUES

There's a broad range of outdoor medical issues, many of which can be prevented. This brief outline describes the most common. Keep in mind that kids are different from adults in a variety of anatomic and physiologic ways. For example, their smaller size makes them more at risk for problems like animal envenomization and dehydration. They have a less developed immune system, which means it takes them more energy to fight off illness. Although their growing bones often heal readily, a fracture near the growing part of a bone can be potentially debilitating. Finally, children have more difficulty regulating their temperature. They can get too cold or too hot much more quickly than adults for a variety of reasons, such as a larger surface-area-to-mass ratio, less behavioral adaptation, lack of sweating and fat, and inability to dissipate heat or ward off cold.

Dehydration

Kids are more susceptible to dehydration because they forget to drink. Encourage fluid consumption. A good gauge for their fluid status is to check their urine. If it is copious and clear, they are well hydrated. If it is scant and dark yellow, they are likely dehydrated.

Dehydration can be classified as follows:

- Mild: alert, moist or slightly dry eyes or mouth, thirst
- Moderate: restless and irritable, rapid heart rate and breathing, sunken eyes, dry eyes and mouth, minimal dark yellow urine
- Severe: lethargy, cool and mottled skin, severe rapid heart rate and breathing, dry eyes and mouth, no urine output

Treatment for dehydration in the field for kids is oral rehydration solution (ORS). The most convenient ORS comes as a premixed powder that you add to a water bottle. Alternatively, Gatorade or half-strength juice with a pinch of salt works okay. You can make ORS using the following recipe from the World Health Organization: 1 teaspoon salt, 1 cup rice cereal, 1 quart water. Remember to monitor urine output, quantity, and color.

Cold-Temperature Illness

At all seasons, especially in winter, kids can succumb to hypothermia or frostbite. Hypothermia is when the body temperature cools. Frostbite is a condition in which the skin actually freezes. Sometimes kids can have both together. Always keep your kids warm to prevent both. In winter, they should have proper warm clothing and should cover up exposed skin. If boating or snorkeling, they need a wetsuit for cold water. If camping, bring a warm tent and sleeping bag at night.

Observe your kids closely for signs of early hypothermia, such as shivering, lethargy, incoordination, difficulty speaking, dizziness, and decreased energy level. Have drinking water and snacks available, since good nutrition and hydration can help prevent hypothermia. Keep a change of clothes handy when swimming is finished, especially if you are camping or if you have a long drive home. Signs of frostbite include cold, white patches of exposed skin and numbness or tingling in affected fingers and toes.

Below are some tips to prevent hypothermia and frostbite; you can use these items to warm up kids when they are cold too.

- Use layers, including next-to-skin polypropylene underwear, middle layers of bulky fleece, and an outer windproof, waterproof parka. Dress your children the same way you dress yourself.
- Put on extra clothes before kids start shivering.
- Put on rain gear before they are wet.

- Use a hat, neck gaiter, scarf, gloves or mittens, goggles, and other accessories.
- Use durable, good-quality socks and boots that are waterproof.
- Seek shelter from wind, snow, and rain.
- Insulate from the ground when taking breaks using a sleeping pad or backpack.
- Get in a sleeping bag with an adult to warm up quickly.
- Eat carbohydrates, which are quickly and easily absorbed.
- Drink plenty of fluids, preferably an electrolyte solution like a sport drink. Remember, kids get warm from drinking hot chocolate because of the sugar, which gives them extra calories, not from the warmth of the liquid. It should be lukewarm, not hot.
- Consider using chemical hot packs, but don't put them directly on kids' skin.

Heat Illnesses

Heat illness, heat exhaustion, or heat stroke can be life threatening, especially in kids, so prevention is vital. Always dress your child for sun and heat using long-sleeve, long-leg, light-colored cotton clothing if at the beach or in hot climates. Also, keep him or her well hydrated.

If your child gets too hot, find shade, fan your child, and use cool moist towels under armpits, on the forehead, or in the groin. Be careful if you soak your child's clothing with water; he or she may cool too rapidly, and the weather may change. Avoid cooling below the 100-degree core body temperature. Just cool the child down so he or she feels better and the body temperature drops to 100 degrees. Check his or her temperature, if you have a thermometer.

Sunburn

Whether you're in the pool or at the beach, sun safety is vital, as discussed in chapter 2. A brief reminder:
- Wear a swimsuit that covers up as much of the torso as possible, such as a long-sleeve T-shirt made from Lycra and shorts.
- Avoid peak hours between 10 A.M. and 2 P.M., when the sun's rays are most intense.
- Always apply waterproof sunscreen of 25 SPF or greater. Remember, apply it liberally and often. Use a golf-ball-sized glob for a fifty-pound child.
- If you are at the beach or an outdoor pool, make your child wear a sun hat and sunglasses.

Drowning

Drowning is something parents fear, and with good reason. Drowning is the third most common cause of accidental death among children under four years old. It is very easy to prevent in most swim settings, such as a pool or lake: Supervise your kids. The easiest way to do this is to get in the water with them. Too many times I've seen parents at the side of the lake watching. Not only is it more fun to get in the water with your kids, it's much easier to keep an eye on them or react quickly if necessary.

If you are at the scene of a near-drowning, the chief focus is on respiratory resuscitation. Over 90 percent of near-drowning victims survive with CPR at the scene. This is a great reason to take a Small Hearts CPR course to learn this important skill.

Minor Trauma

Minor cuts and scrapes are probably the most common injury among kids. They will fall and get hurt. There are many injuries that can occur at the beach or at your local swimming hole. Cuts and scrapes can occur from logs, rocks, and seashells, and they can get infected. Have your children wear shoes in and out of the water to prevent cuts on their feet. Old canvas tennis shoes or sport sandals work well. If you are beachcombing, try rubber boots. Also, watch for marine creatures such as crabs, jellyfish, or barnacles at the beach.

The mainstay of treatment is good wound care. To clean wounds, follow this step-by-step algorithm.

1. Wash your hands.
2. Remove any major stones or dirt.
3. Wash the wound thoroughly with a skin cleanser and clean water.
4. Irrigate with a syringe if you have one. This removes even more germs.
5. Dress with a small amount of first aid ointment.
6. Cover with a bandage that is larger than the wound. For large wounds, use gauze and first aid tape.
7. Once a bandage is applied, you may have to cover the dressing with a second layer, such as an Ace wrap or gauze roll, to keep it clean.

Animal Bites

Animal bites can be disastrous, both cosmetically disfiguring and life threatening. Prevent animal bites by teaching your children safety: Look where you step or reach, avoid holes and crevices, and wear good boots and long pants. Always supervise your kids.

Rattlesnake and scorpion bites are perhaps the most dangerous for kids.

Treatment is good wound care and immobilization. For example, if they are bitten in the arm, put the arm in a sling. If in the leg, carry them.

Poisonous snakes include pit vipers like rattlesnakes and cottonmouths. Many hospitals carry pit viper antivenin, especially those where rattlesnakes are indigenous. The bark scorpion inhabits Arizona and other parts of the Southwest and can sting a victim with venom. Arizona hospitals carry antivenin.

Stings and Bites from Insects and Arthropods

Insect and spider bites are very common. Bee sting allergic shock is the biggest threat. If you know your child is allergic to bees, wasps, or any other relatives of the Hymenoptera family, carry an allergic bee sting kit such as the EpiPen or EpiPen Jr. The kit should have both epinephrine and diphenhydramine.

Ticks are common too. They attach to the skin for a couple hours before burrowing, so check your kids' skin often if you are traveling in tick-infested areas, and remove ticks promptly. Prevention is best done by wearing long-sleeve shirts and long pants. Tuck pants into socks. Ticks can envenomate or transmit bacteria if they burrow in skin. Good wound care is important after removal.

Mosquitoes and other biting insects can be thwarted by covering skin also. Use mosquito nets, hats, scarves, long-sleeve shirts, and long pants. If you want to use repellent on your kids, citronella is less toxic than DEET, which is absorbed systemically. There are several commercial preparations for kids. Remember malaria prophylaxis if you are traveling to an endemic area.

Contact Dermatitis

Contact dermatitis is a skin irritation from poison oak, ivy, or sumac or many other less-toxic plants. Prevent a bad rash by covering skin, again with long sleeves and long pants. Technu is a commercial solution that neutralizes toxins from poison oak and ivy. Use it as a preventive measure after your child comes in contact with the plant.

International Travel

International travel has many risks, especially in developing countries. Some important issues with air travel include eustachian tube (ear canal) dysfunction and motion sickness. This is most easily prevented by having your child suck on candy, chew gum, or drink from a bottle during takeoff and landings. Diphenhydramine may help with motion sickness.

Traveler's diarrhea is another common ailment. For diarrhea, Pepto Bismol may help. Antimotility agents should be used with caution, especially with fever or blood in the stool. Empiric antibiotic treatment for children is possible. Talk to your doctor ahead of time.

For further health issues related to international travel, check internet sources such as:

- Centers for Disease Control: www.cdc.gov/travel
- World Health Organization: www.who.int/ith/index.html
- International Association for Medical Assistance to Travelers: www.iamat.org

FIRST AID KITS

You can buy an adult first aid kit from your local outdoor or camping store. Try to find one designed for families. Alternatively, use an adult outdoor first aid kit as the basis and add certain items geared specifically toward kids. If you want to buy a zippered pouch and build your own, I've listed two types of first aid kits, beginning with a comprehensive family kit. This may stay in your car but will also work great for boat or backpacking trips. If you have special needs, such as when traveling to the tropics, to a developing country, or to high altitudes, you may need more specific medicines or equipment. A bare-bones first aid kit is listed last. This is something small enough to keep in your fanny pack, backpack, or bike seat bag. It has minimal equipment for basic wound care.

BASIC FAMILY FIRST AID KIT

Medicines	Use
Acetaminophen: drops, liquid, chewable	Treat fever or pain
Ibuprofen: liquid, chewable	Treat fever, swelling, or pain
Diphenhydramine: liquid or tablets	Treat allergies
Charcoal, powdered	Neutralize ingested toxic substance like poisonous plants or camping fuel
Ipecac syrup	Make child vomit ingested toxic substance
Epinephrine, EpiPen	Treat allergic shock
Oral antibiotics, suspension or tabs	Treat infections (according to your doctor's recommendations)
Oral Rehydration Solution, powdered	Treat dehydration

BASIC FAMILY FIRST AID KIT *continued*

Medicines	Use
Diaper cream, A&D or Desitin	Treat rash
Sting-relief swabs	Treat insect bites or stings
Kids' sunscreen	Provide sun protection
Kids' insect repellent	Prevent insect bites

Equipment	Use
Thermometer	Take temperature
Syringe	Dispense medicine or clean wounds
Small forceps	Remove splinters
Safety pins	Multiple uses

Bandages/Wound Care	Use
Antiseptic towelettes	Clean hands
Waterless hand gel	Clean hands
Antibiotic ointment	Treat wounds
Wound cleaning soap	Cleanse wounds
Character bandages	Cover minor wounds
Butterfly bandages	Cover minor wounds
Cloth first aid tape	Many uses
Gauze squares (two or four inch)	Cover large wounds

MINIMALIST FIRST AID KIT

Contents	Use
Cloth first aid tape	Cover wounds
Povidone-iodine wipe	Clean wounds
Steristrips, large	Close minor cuts
Benzoin crush tube	Keep Steristrips on skin
Band-Aids	Cover wounds
Sunscreen	Prevent sunburn
Bio-occlusive dressing	Keep wounds covered
Gauze squares (four-by-four inch)	Stop bleeding
Gauze roll	Cover larger wounds

◇ **18** ◇

Survival Kits for Kids and Parents

When I helped teach an avalanche and survival skills course for snowboarders a few years back, students had a rare opportunity to see what was inside the instructors' packs. After I tore mine apart, piece by piece, I was eager to see what my fellow wilderness educators carried. All of us had common items and wildly different ones, especially with regard to survival, first aid, and repair gear. Years previous, I had embraced the "light is right" maxim; by unloading my pack and looking at others', I critically reevaluated my gear and shed even more ounces.

I'd recommend that parents adhere to this too. Take the basic survival gear, but don't overdo it. You have enough to deal with just being a parent. But if you ever get into a survival situation, you'll be happy you had some basic gear.

I tend to have a basic survival kit that stows in a one-quart freezer bag. These bags are tough and light, and you can see through them. The kit easily fits in a fanny pack, day pack, or the pocket of my parka. This mandates that I keep it small, for if it is too heavy or bulky, I may not bring it for a quick two-hour hike or bike ride.

The kit is designed for short trips. For longer trips, I take more stuff, especially a larger first aid kit and more extensive survival supplies for my car. You can buy some commercially available emergency/survival kits, but many of us prefer to prepare our own custom-made kit.

You probably will customize your own kit depending on your willingness to carry weight, your activity, and any special needs. Kids can take some variation of this. Young kids might simply take a whistle and a pocket radio. Older kids will like carrying a map and compass as well as a basic first aid kit. Don't forget, in addition to this gear you'll need extra food, water, and clothing.

EMERGENCY SURVIVAL KIT FOR PARENTS

- Matches, windproof and waterproof in watertight jar with striking swatch (Alternatively, consider a metal match, which is a piece of flint with a metal striker.)
- Compass, with declination correction
- Map
- Batteries, 2 extra
- Chemical hand/foot warmers, 2
- Perlon cord, 10 feet by 4mm
- Whistle
- Headlamp or flashlight

- Chemical heat packs
- Multitool (The tiny SwissTool has pliers, a wire cutter, and screwdrivers.)
- Pocket knife (key-chain-size knife with a blade, scissors, screwdriver, and tweezers)
- Duct tape, 2 inch by 5 feet (rolled, then squeezed flat)
- Paper clips, 2 (for wire)
- Safety pins, 2
- Plastic cable ties, 2, or stretchy polyurethane plastic straps

EMERGENCY KIT FOR KIDS

- Bandages
- Whistle
- FRS radio

- Compass
- Map
- First aid tape

- First aid and survival booklet

EXTRA ITEMS FOR YOUR CAR

- Spare food, water, clothing
- Blanket
- Spare tire, jack, tire iron, basic repair tools
- Tow strap or heavy rope
- Flares or reflective triangles
- Compact shovel and saw

- Headlamp or flashlight with extra batteries
- Work gloves
- Spare raincoat/boots
- Car first aid kit
- Sunscreen

Index

About the Author

Christopher Van Tilburg's parents taught him to ski when he was seven years old. He grew up hunting, fishing, canoeing, hiking, and traveling the world. He now teaches his own daughters, Skylar and Avrie, to ski, climb, hike, bike, swim, and camp.

He works as an emergency physician and as a mountain rescue doctor. He serves as Editor-in-Chief for *Wilderness Medicine* magazine, as a board member of Wilderness Medical Society, and as a medical committee member of Mountain Rescue Association.

BOOKS

Backcountry Snowboarding
Canyoneering: Beginning to Advanced Techniques
Backcountry Ski Oregon: Classic Descents for Skiers and Snowboarders,
*   Including Southwest Washington*
Emergency Survival: A Pocket Guide
First Aid: A Pocket Guide
Watersports Safety and Emergency First Aid: A Handbook for Boaters, Anglers,
*   Kayakers, River Runners, and Surfriders*

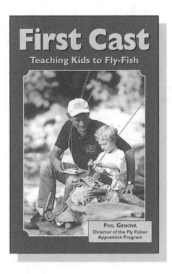

Our editors recommend . . .